Henry: Portrait of a Serial Killer

✖ Controversies

Series editors: Stevie Simkin and Julian Petley

Controversies is a series comprising individual studies of controversial films from the late 1960s to the present day, encompassing classic, contemporary Hollywood, cult and world cinema. Each volume provides an in-depth study analysing the various stages of each film's production, distribution, classification and reception, assessing both its impact at the time of its release and its subsequent legacy.

Also published

Stevie Simkin, *Straw Dogs*

Neal King, *The Passion of the Christ*

Peter Krämer, *A Clockwork Orange*

Forthcoming

Lucy Burke, *The Idiots*

Gabrielle Murray, *Bad Boy Bubby*

Jude Davies, *Falling Down*

Julian Petley, *Crash*

Stevie Simkin, *Basic Instinct*

'The *Controversies* series is a valuable contribution to the ongoing debate about what limits – if any – should be placed on cinema when it comes to the depiction and discussion of extreme subject matter. Sober, balanced and insightful where much debate on these matters has been hysterical, one-sided and unhelpful, these books should help us get a perspective on some of the thorniest films in the history of cinema.'
Kim Newman, novelist, critic and broadcaster

Henry: Portrait of a Serial Killer

Shaun Kimber

© Shaun Kimber 2011

First published 2011 by
PALGRAVE MACMILLAN

PALGRAVE MACMILLAN in the UK is an imprint of Macmillan Publishers
Limited, registered in England, company number 785998, of Houndmills,
Basingstoke, Hampshire RG21 6XS.

Palgrave Macmillan in the US is a division of St Martin's Press LLC,
175 Fifth Avenue, New York, NY 10010.

Palgrave Macmillan is the global academic imprint of the above companies
and has companies and representatives throughout the world.

Palgrave® and Macmillan® are registered trademarks in the United States,
the United Kingdom, Europe and other countries

ISBN: 978–0–230–29798–2

A catalogue record for this book is available from the British Library.

A catalog record for this book is available from the Library of Congress.

10   9   8   7   6   5   4   3   2   1
20   19   18   17   16   15   14   13   12   11

Printed in China

For Keri, Margaret and Barry

Contents

Part 1: *Henry: Portrait of a Serial Killer* Then

Part 2: *Henry: Portrait of a Serial Killer* since Then

✗ Introduction

'HE'S NOT FREDDY, HE'S NOT JASON … HE'S REAL'

This book will explore why *Henry: Portrait of a Serial Killer* (1986) has generated controversy for an extended period of time and in several countries. *Henry*[1] was the first independent feature film to be directed by John McNaughton and was produced in Chicago, Illinois in 1985. It is a fictional character study based on the real-life crimes of American serial killer Henry Lee Lucas, whose story also inspired *Confessions of a Serial Killer* (1987), a film that has been overshadowed by the controversy surrounding its predecessor, and *Drifter: Henry Lee Lucas* (2009) (aka *Henry Lee Lucas: Serial Killer*). *Henry* was produced during the 1980s but did not achieve mainstream distribution and exhibition until the early 1990s. This gap makes *Henry* an interesting case study because it proved to be a significant factor in the longevity of the controversy linked to the film. The promotional copy on the back of the 2001 UK Universal Pictures DVD release proclaims it to be 'one of the most controversial films of all time', and the controversy has been fuelled and fanned by a range of players including the film-makers, marketers, the press, film critics, censors and audiences. Whilst recognising that controversies are historically contingent, culturally specific, constantly in flux, overlapping and cyclical rather than linear, in the case of *Henry* certain issues and themes do recur in a range of contexts and across time. As Henry[2] himself says of murder, controversies are 'always the same and it's always different'.

This book examines the impact that this controversy continues to have upon the regulation, censorship and classification of *Henry* in the US and the UK.[3] Building upon a revisionist perspective, the book examines how the ongoing regulation and censorship of *Henry* draws upon a complex, dynamic and relational set of discourses, practices and apparatus, which produce cultural meanings, reveal social fears and offer glimpses into the operation of regulatory and censorial power (Kimber, 2000; Hendershot, 1998; Thompson, 1997; Jansen, 1991; Kuhn, 1988). Examining film as a social process and cultural experience, and drawing upon a wide range of primary and secondary sources, this case study takes into account the industrial and cultural contexts within which *Henry* was developed, produced, distributed, marketed, exhibited, regulated, censored, critically received and consumed (Turner, 2002; Harbord, 2002).

The overarching reason for the intense debate attaching to *Henry* is the extreme range of responses that it has evoked from viewers. These responses have been generated by a number of overlapping contextual, textual and intertextual factors, which are the focus of this book. In summing up his chapter on *Henry*, James Marriott states that '*Henry's* non-judgmental tone and lack of redemption or punishment make it an easier film to admire than enjoy' (2004, p. 293). This sentiment is borne out when considering reactions to *Henry* by audiences, reviewers, regulators and academics. Responses to the film have often been framed by a mixture of revulsion and admiration. The most negative reactions often centre on the belief that the film offers no 'moral compass' or explanation for Henry's actions; presents disturbing violence as entertainment; encourages viewers uncritically to identify with the killer; adopts a confrontational and inaccessible tone; and confirms stereotypical attitudes about the underprivileged (Hallam and Marshment, 2000). Standpoints characterized by admiration often cite the honesty and intensity of the film, its serious and unglamorous examination of cinematic violence, its meta-fictional reflection on the pleasures of film violence and its challenge to the orthodoxy of Hollywood films (Falsetto, 2000; Hallam and Marshment, 2000). Characteristics that elicit admiration and praise from one observer often prompt distaste and condemnation from another. Moreover, responses to *Henry* often commingle revulsion and appreciation. For example, in his review of *Henry*, Roger Ebert (1990) notes that the film was 'too violent and disgusting to be endured' by many viewers, but that the film deals 'honestly with its subject matter'. This point is reinforced by bob the moo's (2007) post in user comments on *Henry* on the Internet Movie Database (IMDB):

> Is it a brilliant film? No, no it isn't but I can only assume that those who have dismissed it as 'not scary' or 'not violent enough' or 'boring' are simply missing the strengths that the film has while highlighting the failings in areas where it never purports to be strong. Violent but unglamorous, engaging but repulsive – I'll not rush to watch it again but it is an important film worth seeing once.

This tension in responses to *Henry* helps to position its centrality within debates around controversial film within the late twentieth and early twenty-first centuries.

Martin Rubin suggests that these polarized responses result from the film being an 'exercise in purposeful confusion' and 'instability' (1992, pp. 54, 57), and that films within this small sub-subgenre of modern multiple-murder films, which include *Henry*, offer a wide variety of signs that are not easily readable. He holds that the stylistic and structural devices within these films, in terms of how the material is presented, how the spectator is positioned and the films' relationships to other films, make them difficult to decipher. As Philip L. Simpson argues:

> Watching this film presents the genre conscious viewer with a number of false starts and red herrings, creating an uncertainty that is crucial to McNaughton's insistence that signs cannot be reliably read. Just as Henry evades detection, the film eludes easy analysis or categorisation. (2000, p. 148)

Such a reading strategy, which seeks out the 'portrait' offered by the film's title, is likely to lead to frustration and alienation as a result of the film deliberately setting up a system of tensions and contradictions without refining, developing or resolving them (Rubin, 1992, p. 54). In other words, viewers of *Henry* have to work hard to make sense of a film in which it is deliberately made difficult to forge connections and find explanations, and in which no resolutions are offered. We are actively encouraged to come up with our own responses to the film based upon our decoding of the opaque signs in the text, our intertextual reading of the film in light of other films, our extratextual reading of the film within a wider range of social, cultural and political contexts, and also the regimes of knowledge, cultural dispositions, preferences and tastes that we bring to the encounter (Hallam and Marshment, 2000; Sconce, 1993). As Rubin points out, 'it is difficult for the spectator to find a place to stand in these films' (1992, p. 56). And it is precisely for this reason that the film has generated such highly polarized responses, which, in turn, have fuelled, fanned and spread the controversy surrounding *Henry* over the last twenty-five years and across different territories.

The book explores a range of issues linked to this ongoing controversy. Part 1 explores *Henry's* development, pre-production, production and post-production, a journey that laid the foundations for the later furore. This is followed by an examination of *Henry's* struggle to gain theatrical distribution in the US as a result of the stigmatizing and commercially prohibitive 'X' rating issued by the Motion Picture Association of America (MPAA); it concludes with an outline of the film's initial critical reception in the US. Part 2 examines *Henry's* wrangles with the British Board of Film Classification (BBFC) in the UK, culminating in its belated and censored 1991 theatrical release. This account traces the continuing controversy over *Henry* within the British context, focusing upon the critical reception of the 1991 theatrical release, the delayed, censored and re-edited 1993 video release, the less censored 2001 video release and the 2003 re-releases of uncut theatrical and DVD versions of the film. Part 2 also investigates the ongoing commodification of *Henry* through successive American and UK re-releases on DVD including the 20th Anniversary Special Edition in 2005. Part 3 examines various intersecting ideas, issues and themes that help to explain why *Henry* has remained so controversial for so long and in so many countries. Amongst the topics explored are context (overlapping contexts, film violence and the serial-killer subgenre), text (narrative, visual style and debates linked to realism and authenticity), and audience (viewers' emotional responses). Part 4 subjects three scenes to close textual analysis, scenes singled out because of their centrality to the debate provoked by the film as expressed in various related regulatory, critical, academic, audience, production and marketing discourses. Part 5 draws together the overarching themes of the book, advances a model for the analysis of controversial films in general, and considers the ongoing legacy of *Henry* within contemporary film cultures.

✕ Synopsis

Henry (Michael Rooker) is an ex-convict who has served time for the murder of his mother, committed when he was fourteen. He works as an exterminator but his vocation is serial murder, as he drives around Chicago looking for potential victims. Henry shares a flat with Otis[4] (Tom Towles), a paroled ex-convict whom he met in prison and who now works at Bob's Gas. Otis supplements his wages by dealing drugs. Becky (Tracy Arnold), Otis's sister and a former nightclub dancer, comes to stay. She has a daughter, Lurlean, and an abusive husband, Leroy, who is in prison for murder. Becky wants to move to Chicago to make a new start, to find work, escape Leroy and bring up Lurlean.

Becky and Henry develop a rapport during a game of cards in which they share experiences of childhood familial abuse. When Becky asks Henry if he killed his mother, he explains how he did so but tells more than one version of the story. Becky points this out to him. Whilst attracted to Becky, Henry is uncomfortable with the feelings this generates, so keeps his distance and maintains a closer relationship with Otis. Becky gets a job as a shampoo girl at Fox Hair. After a meal Henry challenges Otis's incestuous advances towards his sister. To defuse the situation, Becky suggests that they go out for a drink. Whilst out they pick up two prostitutes (Mary Demas and Kristin Finger), whom Henry murders in front of Otis in an alleyway. Otis, who had initially been shocked, is introduced to Henry's philosophy of killing: 'It's always the same and it's always different … it's either you or them one way or another', and soon becomes an enthusiastic apprentice.

After Otis kicks in a television in their apartment, he and Henry go shopping for a new one. They visit a fence (Ray Atherton) and, following an argument, kill him by stabbing him, strangling him, smashing a TV on his head and then turning it on. Back at the apartment Henry, Otis and Becky video themselves dancing with the equipment stolen from the fence. Following an interview with his parole officer (Eric Young), Otis meets a male high-school student (Kurt Naebig) to carry out a drug deal. His sexual advances towards the student having been violently rejected, he returns to his apartment and tells Henry that he would like to kill the student. However, Henry instructs him not to take out his anger on someone who could so easily be linked back to him. They go for a drive and, pretending to have broken down, Henry flags down a motorist (Rick Paul). Handing Otis a gun, he invites his friend to shoot the motorist, which Otis duly does.

Whilst filming a fight between a group of homeless men in a park and driving around Chicago, Henry instructs Otis on how to avoid police detection by killing randomly with no distinctive *modus operandi* and by keeping mobile. Later, they invade a middle-class suburban home and kill the son (Sean Ores), wife (Lisa Temple) and husband (Brian Graham) whilst recording the murders on the stolen video camera. During the invasion, Henry challenges Otis over his sexual molestation of the dead mother. Back in their apartment, the pair watch the video, and Henry is alarmed when Otis rewinds the tape to watch it again in slow motion. Later the camera breaks whilst they are driving around filming women. They argue before Henry leaves Otis in downtown Chicago and drives off.

Henry returns to the apartment, where Becky tells him that she misses her daughter and has quit her job. She asks Henry to go back with her to her mother's place. Henry says that he will think about it and then offers to take Becky out for a steak dinner. When they return, Henry finds Otis passed out on the couch with the home-invasion video playing in slow motion on the television; he removes the tape. Becky returns from the bathroom and invites Henry into her room. In the bedroom Becky tries to kiss Henry. An uncomfortable Henry is further startled when Otis walks in on them. He goes for a walk to clear his head, buys some cigarettes and chats to a woman walking her dog (Donna Dunlap).

The bloody suitcase dumped on the side of a road at the end of *Henry*.

He returns to find Otis raping and strangling Becky and is overpowered by Otis when he tries to intervene. Becky stabs Otis in the eye with the handle of a metal comb, and Henry finishes him off with the comb before dismembering his body in the bathroom. After throwing Otis's remains off a bridge, Henry and Becky drive to Sunset Motel for the night. En route, Becky tells Henry that she loves him and he says he guesses that he loves her too. In the morning Henry shaves, packs his belongings into the car and drives off alone. He stops at the side of a road, takes a bloody suitcase from the boot of the car, dumps it and drives away.

✖ Part 1

HENRY: PORTRAIT OF A SERIAL KILLER THEN

This chapter explores *Henry*'s production history within the wider context of the emerging US video industry, and suggests that *Henry*'s journey laid the foundations for the later controversy surrounding the film. The chapter also examines *Henry*'s attempts to gain theatrical distribution in the US and charts its initial critical reception as a way of understanding how the dynamic and productive processes of circulation, classification, marketing, advertising and reception impacted upon debate about the film. Issues linked to the contexts within which *Henry* was produced, circulated and received are considered in more detail in Part 3.

Director John McNaughton was born on 13 January 1950 to working-class parents, and was raised on Chicago's industrial South Side. Growing up in the 1950s and 1960s, television and film were major influences upon him. McNaughton spent two years at the University of Illinois studying sculpture, and in 1969 he moved to Chicago's Columbia College where he majored in film and television and minored in photography. After graduating in 1972 there was little work available in media production so he worked in a number of factories and then in the audiovisual department of an advertising agency. Following a separation from his wife, feeling frustrated with his life, he joined the Royal American Show – a travelling carnival – and toured Canada and America, taking still photos along the way. During 1975 McNaughton moved to New Orleans where he worked as a silversmith and then built sailing boats before moving into construction. He returned to Chicago in 1978 to start a career in film, moving in with his parents and working in his cousin's bar, Lassons Tap. A theme common to several of McNaughton's commentaries on his early career is that, following a period of confinement after graduation, he escaped to embrace the free spirit of the 1960s before deciding towards the end of the 1970s to start a career in film.

According to McNaughton, one day in his cousin's bar, a man who worked for Maljack (later Maljack Productions Incorporated, hereafter referred to as MPI) gave him his business card. MPI was an early independent audiovisual business based in Illinois that was run by the Jordanian brothers, Waleed B. Ali and Malik B. Ali. The Ali brothers bought public-domain footage (copyright-free) and projected it in these pre-domestic video days on Super 8 loops in nostalgia-themed restaurants. They also set up 16mm projectors and rented films. McNaughton started a job for MPI, delivering equipment, but left to return to construction work. Whilst at MPI, McNaughton and the Ali brothers had talked about how video would eventually take off; how films would be made for video; and how they would make a film together for video distribution. And during the early 1980s video did indeed take off, and the Ali brothers started buying the rights to films for video distribution.

Development

McNaughton later revisited the Ali brothers and met with Ray Atherton (who plays the fence in *Henry*). Atherton was a film collector and an expert on public-domain material, and he and McNaughton collaborated on a documentary on American gangsters, using public-domain footage: MPI distributed the documentary, *Dealers in Death* (1984), on video. Thanks to its success, McNaughton started working with MPI on a video documentary using vintage film of professional wrestling from the 1950s. However, when the owners of the wrestling footage increased their asking price, the deal fell through. In August 1985, whilst McNaughton was working remodelling Burger King joints, Waleed B. Ali offered him the $100,000 budget originally meant for the wrestling video. As McNaughton recollects: 'I walked into Waleed's office that day expecting to commence production on a wrestling documentary.[5] I walked out with a deal to make my first real film' (2003a, p. 1). During the early 1980s, horror titles were financially important within the emerging video market, to the point that acquiring the rights to distribute them was becoming increasingly expensive. This prompted MPI to strategize a move into production, which would give them the rights for all markets worldwide. Waleed, who commissioned the film, wanted a horror film but did not care what the subject matter was (Jarecki, 2001). It is a rare privilege amongst first-time directors, even independents, to have the chance to conceive, develop and complete a work according to their own vision.

McNaughton had a budget and a brief; now all he needed was an idea for the film. As he left the meeting he went to speak to an old friend of his who worked for MPI, Gus Kavooras. According to McNaughton, Gus was 'a collector and connoisseur of the arcane and offbeat' and he said to him: 'Waleed just offered me $100,000 to make a horror movie. I have no idea what to make' (Falsetto, 2000, p. 324). Gus pulled out a videotape of the television news show *20/20*, which featured a segment about the US serial killers Henry Lee Lucas and Ottis Elwood Toole, and it was this which initiated the idea for *Henry*. McNaughton was interested in the background of Henry Lee Lucas and also found his creepy but personable manner intriguing. Although McNaughton was interested in real-life crime, he had apparently never before come across the term 'serial killer' (Falsetto, 2000).

Henry Lee Lucas was born 23 August 1938 in Virginia, and was brought up in a deprived and abusive environment. On 12 January 1960 he murdered his mother, Viola. He was eventually charged with second-degree murder and sentenced to between twenty and forty years in prison, although in June 1970, because of overcrowding, he was released. In 1977, living in Florida, Henry met Ottis Elwood Toole, whose childhood had also been characterised by poverty and abuse. From 1978 Henry and Ottis were involved in a range of robberies, arson attacks, rapes and murders, the most infamous of these incidents being the murder of an unidentified woman known as 'Orange Socks'. Henry (now forty years' old) fell for Ottis's niece Becky Powell (who was thirteen), which caused a rift between Ottis and Henry, because Ottis was in love with Henry. Henry and Ottis parted company in January 1982 and, towards the end of August that year, Henry killed Becky after she tried to leave him. He also raped and killed Kate Rich, with whom he and Becky had stayed. Henry was eventually arrested for possession of a firearm, and on 1 October 1983 he pleaded guilty to the murder of Kate Rich, receiving a seventy-five-year sentence. On 10 October he was sentenced to life imprisonment for the murder of Becky, and then claimed responsibility for the rape and murder of 'Orange Socks'. Henry was sentenced to death because the murder had been accompanied by another serious offence. Encouraged by law-enforcement agencies that were keen to clear up as many unsolved murders as possible, Henry confessed to numerous crimes, but later retracted these confessions. Ottis died in prison in September 1996. In June 1998 Henry's death sentence was commuted to life imprisonment by the then Governor of Texas, George W. Bush, because of doubts over his guilt in the 'Orange Socks' case. Henry died from a heart attack in prison on 12 March 2001. He was sixty-four.

McNaughton, whilst conversant with post-production video, had no experience in the film industry. He had a budget and an idea but needed a writer. A first attempt collaborating with Gus Kavooras did not work out and, keen to shoot before the winter set in, McNaughton took the idea to an old friend and colleague, Steven A. Jones, a musician, designer and commercial animation director who was well connected in Chicago's film-making community. Jones would become one of the film's producers and its post-production supervisor, as well as directing and helping to compose the original music. Jones put McNaughton in touch with the Organic Theatre Company (OTC), one of Chicago's top off-Broadway groups, which had been formed by Stuart Gordon of *Re-Animator* (1985) fame. Through the group McNaughton met Richard Fire (co-scriptwriter and acting coach on *Henry*), who was at a loose end after the script for the OTC production *ER* had been sold to an American TV network. McNaughton had a straightforward exploitation film in mind but Fire felt that more could be done with the concept. Beginning in August 1985, they co-wrote the script for *Henry* over a period of a couple of months, basing it upon research material about Henry Lee Lucas in particular and serial killers in general, and creating a fictional dramatization of events taken from the mediated retelling of 'stories' which Henry Lee Lucas had retracted in prison. This blending of fact and fiction provoked controversy by tapping into the overlapping ideological, social, cultural, political, legal and economic concerns surrounding serial killers – an issue that will be returned to in more detail in Part 3.

McNaughton and Fire sought simultaneously to redefine and push at the boundaries of horror film through the merging of what in cinematic terms we might call art and exploitation cinema. As McNaughton put it: 'If our charge was to make a horror film, we made it our objective to horrify an audience to the maximum degree possible' (2003a, p. 2). Their vision for *Henry* involved removing the buffer of fantasy which allows audiences to experience film violence at a safe and comfortable distance; encouraging viewers to question the spectacle of film violence as entertainment whilst implicating film-makers and audiences within this process; taking spectators into the everyday life of a serial killer and encouraging them to identify and sympathize with him; refusing to offer a moral compass by means of which to judge Henry or the film; presenting a human monster who exists next to us in the real world; and breaking the illusion that the world is a safe place by having Henry elude the police. McNaughton and Fire made it an integral part of their vision of *Henry* that the film would push boundaries, and they knew that this would court controversy.

Pre-production

McNaughton gave Waleed Ali a copy of the screenplay in autumn 1985 and, although he did not read it, he did write a cheque for $25,000 in order to enable pre-production to start. McNaughton used his loft apartment on Milwaukee Avenue as the production office, this being managed by Lisa Dedmond (co-producer and production manager), who was in charge of the finances and whose job it was to ensure that the film came in on budget. Producer Steve Jones brought Charlie Lieberman (director of photography), Rick Paul (art director), Patricia Hart (wardrobe), Robert McNaughton and Ken Hale (original music) to the project. Frank Coronado was enlisted to storyboard 110 panels which represented key scenes in the film,[6] as the budget would not stretch to a shot-by-shot storyboard. Coronado also played a cameo as a 'Bum' in *Henry* and storyboarded McNaughton's *The Borrower* (1991), *Mad Dog and Glory* (1993) and *Normal Life* (1996).

Steve Jones's contacts through the OTC helped with casting. Tommy Towles (*Halloween* (2007), *House of 1000 Corpses* (2003), *Night of the Living Dead* (1990)) an ex-marine with a background in improvisational comedy, read for Henry but was eventually cast as Otis. Towles was one of the original members of the OTC and has since appeared in other McNaughton productions including those mentioned above. Tracy Arnold, who had only recently joined the OTC, was cast as Becky. This was to be her only major film role, although she went on to have small film parts in *The Borrower* and *The Shot* (1996). By an odd coincidence she grew up in Georgetown, Texas, where Lucas was tried. There were some initial problems casting the role of Henry, which attracted little interest from potential actors. McNaughton even considered casting an older actor but had some concerns about his being able to carry off the romantic subplot. Jeffrey Segal (special-effects make-up artist) then recommended Michael Rooker, who would go on to appear in *Sea of Love* (1989), *JFK* (1991), *Cliffhanger* (1993), *The Bone Collector* (1999), *Slither* (2006) and *Jumper* (2008). Rooker had grown up in a welfare family in Jasper, Alabama before moving to Chicago as a child with his father. There he won a scholarship to go to drama school, and, having graduated, by the time he met McNaughton, was working in theatre as well as making ends meet as a painter and decorator in Chicago. Rooker turned up in character to meet McNaughton at Jones's apartment, wearing his painting and decorating clothes. McNaughton recollects: 'He was completely raw and so unlike most of the kids that go into theatre and the arts. After he read for us we offered him a lead role and he accepted' (Jarecki, 2001, p. 197). Indeed, Rooker turned down a part in a play at the prestigious Steppenwolf Theatre to take the lead in *Henry*.

Rooker, Towles and Arnold received $2,000 each for their work on *Henry*, and this included rehearsal time, which consisted of 'table rehearsals' and setting chairs in a room to simulate the set. Rehearsals over a two- to three-week period helped the principal actors develop scenes, establish their characters and build relationships. According to McNaughton: 'Rehearsals are invaluable to get everybody thinking about the movie in the same way. They get comfortable with each other' (Falsetto, 2000, p. 326). After the first meeting with the principal actors, Fire asked them to research their characters and to write their own biographies for them. These were then woven into the script to help tailor the characters to the actors. According to Marriott (2004), the rehearsal time before shooting helped the actors to develop a minimal, semi-improvisational style, which both looks realistic and adds to the documentary feel of the film. For budgetary reasons, *Henry* drew upon unknown theatre actors, friends, volunteers and crew to make up the rest of the cast. For example, colleague Ray Atherton played the fence;[7] friend Monica O'Malley played the mall victim; Erzsebet Sziky, who worked in McNaughton's cousin's bar, played the hitch-hiker; Lisa Temple, who was involved in musical theatre, played the wife in the home-invasion scene; and financier Waleed B. Ali played the store clerk.[8] Non-volunteer day players were paid $100 each. No extras were used: street shots simply featured people who were there at the time. The Screen Actors Guild also agreed to overlook the fact that McNaughton was unable to pay full union rates to his actors because of budgetary constraints. Marriott (2004) suggests that this casting strategy helps to deprive the audience of a certain degree of security by denying them the recognizable faces which would enable them to distance themselves from the film.

McNaughton had no experience of working with actors but felt that he had a good understanding of working-class behaviour and, as a result, was able to obtain naturalistic performances from his cast (Jarecki, 2001). He suggests that his directorial style was to defer to those who knew more than he did and to learn from them, a sentiment echoed in several interviews with some of the principal actors (Gregory, 2005). Michael Rooker stayed in character much of the time and kept himself to himself during production. As he admitted, it was a difficult role but 'I felt like I understood him, I felt like I could pretend to be him and relate to him' (ibid.). And in discussing Tom Towles's performance, McNaughton described it as constituting 'the poetics of idiocy', drawing as it did upon the actor's background in improvised comedy (2003b).

McNaughton is a great fan of Chicago as a city space. His background growing up in and taking photographs of the city enabled him to build up a repertoire of locations suitable for the film. He has also explained (McNaughton and Gregory, 2005a) how his lack of film-making experience meant that he did not pick locations which were conveniently near one another but selected the spaces that would be the best for the film. The small size of the crew and the fact they were working on a flat rate meant they were able to shoot in a large number of locations for *Henry*. McNaughton called in a host of favours, taking advantage of free locations including a friend's apartment block (the 'exterminator' scene) and Waleed B. Ali's newly purchased suburban house (the 'home-invasion' scene). The Chicago locations include Milwaukee Avenue, the Chicago Skyway, Clarke Street, Lower Wacker Drive, North Avenue and West Avenue Bridge.[9]

McNaughton (2003b) has explained how he got a good deal of support from the city of Chicago, as *Henry* was one of the first films originating, being funded and shot there, chiefly in terms of readily granted permits for location shooting. At the time, a permit to shoot in a venue such as Midway Airport cost $50. At one point McNaughton paid the city $110 and ended up closing the busy intersection of Michigan Avenue and Oakes Street for a couple of hours. McNaughton's preference for locations over sets is at its most striking in the scenes in the apartment featured in the film. Otis's apartment was located in a block in the Wicker Park neighbourhood, not far from McNaughton's own apartment. The use of this space for a month cost $700, and, because it was in good repair, Rick Paul had to work hard on the production design, collaborating with Patricia Hart (with whom he had previously worked on theatre projects) to reduce the space and generally dress it down (McNaughton, 2003b). They were both paid a flat rate of $700 for their work on *Henry*.

Production

Marriott (2004) suggests that McNaughton initially envisaged *Henry* being shot in a documentary style, with a handheld camera following a serial killer around for two weeks. But the original cinematographer Jean de Segonzac (*Girls in Prison* (1994), *Normal Life*) had to leave the project before production started, owing to a prior commitment. Ten days before shooting was due to commence, Jones found Charlie Lieberman, who had worked on documentary substance-abuse films in Chicago. The film's visual style – carefully composed and framed shots, naturalistic tone and washed-out colours – came from collaboration between Lieberman and McNaughton. *Henry* was shot in twenty-eight consecutive days between October and November 1985 on 16mm colour negative stock, using Lieberman's own Arriflex 16 SR, and was eventually blown up to 35mm. The home-invasion scene was filmed by Rooker on a borrowed Sony Betamax home video camera until the point at which he puts the camera down, which is when Lieberman took over (see Part 4 for an analysis of this key scene). According to McNaughton, it was whilst watching the dailies at Lieberman's home that he realized that *Henry* could be released theatrically and not just on video as MPI had planned.

    Henry was made with a small crew of multitasking friends made up of Lieberman, Rick Paul and Patricia Hart (when available), two 'all-purpose guys' and, from time to time, Paul Chen (first assistant director) (McNaughton and Gregory, 2005a). Hart would present the actors with a selection of costumes from which they could choose, with her assistance. Sound recordist Thomas Yore often had to work in noisy locations whilst simultaneously operating the boom and the Nagra recorder by himself. There was no money for lighting night exterior shots and locations, but McNaughton (2003b) felt that this added to the naturalistic look of the film. On set the crew had only ten lights. When filming the shooting of the 'Good Samaritan' in Lower Wacker Drive they supplemented the existing fluorescent, green lighting with extra lighting borrowed from a commercial shoot directed by Paul Chen. Production commentaries all make the point that, whilst the film was fun to make, money was extremely tight. The cast and crew were inexperienced; they filmed in some tough locations; days were long; and they regularly had to revise their schedule in the light of issues which arose. As McNaughton points out:

> It's interesting when you start out like that, I didn't know about union crews, it was just 'Here's the work we have to do today,' and we'd shoot until it was done. One time it was twenty-four hours of straight shooting. Everyone was doing it for almost no money. People were on a flat rate for the length of the picture. Thinking back we knew so little about budgeting and scheduling it was like 'Here's $100,000. Okay I'm going to make a movie'. (Falsetto, 2000, p. 325)

Props were often borrowed. The car which Henry drives belonged to a crew member, and at one point they thought they had lost it, which could have entailed reshooting much of the film (McNaughton and Gregory, 2005a). All audiovisual material played on televisions during the film, including an excerpt from *Becket* (1964), was owned by MPI, as there was no money to pay for rights. When asked what he would do differently if he had had a bigger budget, McNaughton often responds that the only thing he would have done was pay people better.

Henry employed five tableaux of six murders. McNaughton suggests that the idea was to show that murder was Henry's vocation and that these are his 'pieces', that this is what he creates through his work (Gregory, 2005). The first tableau was Richard Fire's idea and involved the restaging of a crime-scene photo of the 'Orange Socks' murder seen on a documentary about Henry Lee Lucas. This featured Mary Demas (cast as dead woman, dead prostitute, hooker 1) and was shot in a farmer's field north of Chicago without permission. The second tableau was filmed in McNaughton's cousin's bar enlisting a friend's parents, Elizabeth and Ted Kaden. The third tableau was filmed in a motel and, like the first tableau, featured Mary Demas and was

Fire's idea. (This scene is analysed in Part 4). The fourth tableau, which shows actress Denise Sullivan lying in a river, was shot on Lisa Dedmond's land. The fifth tableau, featuring Monica O'Malley, was again based upon a description of a murder carried out by Henry Lee Lucas; the location chosen was a friend's house in the south suburban area of Chicago.

The special-effects (SFX) work on *Henry* involved a great deal of improvisation. Chicago-based Jeffrey Segal (*Re-Animator*, *Soul Food* (1997)) did most of the SFX work but was assisted by Berndt Rantscheff (*The Borrower*). Rantscheff was also one of the stills photographers, responsible for the mirror shot of Henry that was to be adopted as the poster and cover shot on most publicity and packaging material. There were four main scenes involving SFX make-up work: the controversial third tableau, in which a murdered prostitute is seen with a bottle impaled in her face; the killing of the fence, which involved stabbing him in the hand and body with a soldering iron and

Low-budget SFX – recycling Otis's $700 prosthetic head.

smashing a television on his head; the shooting of the 'Good Samaritan', in which two squibs were employed for the body shots (McNaughton, 2003b; McNaughton and Gregory, 2005b); and the murder of Otis, which involved a $700 prosthetic head. In reference to this last sequence, McNaughton (2003b) describes how they only had one prosthetic eye, which meant that Arnold had to stab it from behind the first time. The head was then recycled as a prop during the decapitation of Otis. As there was not enough money for the multiple costumes needed for gore scenes, Rooker removed his jacket, which was his own, before each of the scenes in the film involving blood.

Post-production

Steve Jones brought Robert McNaughton – no relation to John – to *Henry*. The two of them had already played in bands together, and their objective here was to create a score which was different from most other horror films. Jones played synthesizers and percussion, McNaughton synthesizers and piano, and they wrote the score in collaboration with Ken Hale (synthesizers and piano), who had a small studio and an eight-bit sampler, and Paul Petraitis (guitar, and also stills photographer). Sampling was a new technological development in the music business, and so the integration of manipulated samples of voices and sound effects into the score of *Henry* was, for its time, innovative and experimental. For example, one of Becky's screams was taken off tape, sampled, run backwards and added into the musical score. The samples aurally increase the effectiveness of the film by their stylization, for example, during one tableau we hear the distorted sounds of murder whilst seeing only the aftermath of what is heard. In the scene in which Henry and Otis kill the fence, the sound of a dentist's drill is layered into the soundtrack, whilst in the runup to the home-invasion scene, manipulated screams and dialogue are woven into the soundscape. Dan Haberkorn was responsible for creating background sound effects, which included the sounds of a high-school football practice (whistle and jar), a neck snapping (crumbling a Styrofoam cup near a microphone), and Otis's body being dismembered (ripping a plastic sack). The score cost $2,500. Costs were kept down by recording the score at Time Zone, a new state-of-the-art Chicago-based twenty-four-track studio, which offered the production team a good deal. The studio was run by a born-again rock 'n' roll Christian organization which was later reported to be shocked by the film. The film-makers paid $50 per song for source music, and used local, unsigned bands for tracks such as 'Fingers on It' by Enough Z'Nuff and 'Psycho' by the Sonics.

Steve Jones also brought editor Elena Maganini (editor, sound editor) to *Henry*, and she has since worked with McNaughton on many of his film and TV projects including *Sex, Drugs, Rock & Roll* (1991), *Mad Dog and Glory*, *Normal Life*, *Wild Things* (1998), *Lanksy* (1999) and *Speaking of Sex* (2001). Maganini and McNaughton edited the first cut of *Henry* between November 1985 and June 1996; she had a full-time job cutting animated TV commercials during the day and worked on *Henry* in the evenings and at weekends, setting up a 16mm flatbed editing machine in her apartment. Neither of them had cut a full-length feature before and, as a result, as McNaughton admits, 'you're making it up as you go' (Falsetto, 2000, p. 326). Due to their inexperience the first cut of *Henry* was two and a half hours' long. 'The lesson you never completely learn is that you can't fall in love with every frame' McNaughton remarked, ruefully (Jarecki, 2001, p. 198). Late in the editing process a rough cut was presented to MPI, a decision that McNaughton regrets. There was no budget for a video transfer so he used the Sony video camera employed in the film to record *Henry* off the 16mm flatbed editing machine. This resulted in a copy with a highly degraded, black-and-white, flickering image and a soundtrack minus sound effects. The Ali brothers were appalled and the relationship between them and McNaughton was never the same again. As McNaughton put it: 'They had hoped for horror exploitation, and they felt that the film was terribly made, and worse yet, it was an art film' (ibid.). The brothers demanded: 'Where's the blood and where's the tits? You've made a goddam art film. What are we going to do with this?' (Bouzereau, 2000, p. 201).

MPI owned the rights to the first two Beatles movies, *A Hard Day's Night* (1964) and *Help!* (1965), produced by Walter Shenson. Waleed recommended that McNaughton take the rough cut of *Henry* to Shenson to ask his advice. McNaughton recalls that Shenson told him: 'Yeah kid, that's pretty good but it's way too long. You gotta be ruthless. Anything that you can cut, cut it' (McNaughton and Gregory, 2005b). *Henry* was finished in June 1986 with a running time of eighty-three minutes – sixty-seven minutes had been removed, including a love scene between Henry and Otis, which was felt to be too unbelievable, and a scene in which Becky is attacked in bed while Otis and Henry are out killing two prostitutes. On their return they throw the invader out of the window, which lent the scene an unintentionally comic quality. Also removed were a scene involving Henry fishing, one featuring a street preacher (Neil Flynn – the janitor in *Scrubs*, 2001–10) and a number of tableaux which did not have the desired impact (ibid.).[10]

It has been suggested that the controversy surrounding *Henry* has been built upon and fuelled by various factors, both intentional and unintentional, linked to the film's production history: the blending of fact and fiction, which tapped into wider concerns about serial killers and their representation in films; the provocativeness of the film-makers' vision allied to their lack of budgeting and industrial experience, operating as they were on the edges of mainstream US film-making; the performative realism of the film, created by the casting of unknown actors and the time that the principal actors spent rehearsing, researching and developing their characters; the direction, cinematography and production design, and in particular the extensive location shooting, all of which helped to enhance the perceived realism of the film; gruesome special effects; and a harsh sound mix which drew upon a range of sound effects and at times set up a disturbing dissonance between sound and image. All of these factors contributed to the confrontational nature of *Henry* and helped to establish the foundations upon which much of the attached controversy would be built.

Factoring in post-production costs, MPI felt that it had wasted $111,000 and shelved *Henry*. As McNaughton put it: 'The Ali brothers basically took *Henry* and put it on the shelf and said no one would want to see it' (Jarecki, 2001, p. 198). According to Peter Bates, '*Henry* was an easier film to make than distribute' (1990, p. 56). The chapter will now explore the implications of Bates's contention whilst charting the ongoing debate about the film as it sought distribution in the US.

After finishing *Henry* in June 1986 McNaughton was unemployed for eighteen months. John McDonough points out that 'McNaughton soon learned ... that making an independent film is a cakewalk compared to selling it' (1991, p. 44). As no theatrical release was envisaged by MPI, he had *Henry* transferred onto a one-inch master, colour-corrected video at a transfer lab in Chicago. This meant that he was able to order good-quality video cassettes of the film and circulate them to critics, producers and distributors; these cassettes were often copied or passed on by recipients. McNaughton hand-delivered video cassettes to TV film critics Gene Siskel and Roger Ebert, Michael Medved and Jeffrey Lyons, and press critics such as Elliot Stein. To promote *Henry* further, he made 1,000 handbills headlined 'Yeah, I killed my Momma' and sprayed them with red paint to look like dripping blood. Some of these McNaughton and a friend posted all over the *Chicago Tribune* offices. This would be one of several exploitation methods engaged to raise awareness of and gain grassroots publicity for *Henry* in the runup to finding a distributor.

US Distribution

The first US distributor to show an interest in *Henry* was the major video distribution company Vestron.[11] McNaughton had given a videotape of *Henry* to Steve Hager, editor of the magazine *High Times* in New York, who had a friend at Vestron. A screening was arranged, and Vestron liked *Henry* and offered to buy the film. However, the company proceeded to hold onto it for seven months before deciding not to release it. Two different reasons have been cited for Vestron pulling out. First, legal complications: Vestron's lawyers felt *Henry* was too risky an investment because it used real names and they feared that they might be sued by relatives. Second, Vestron wanted the rights to home-video distribution as well as theatrical distribution whilst MPI wanted to retain the potentially lucrative video rights. Indeed, a recurring feature of the fight to achieve theatrical distribution for *Henry* in the US was the way in which the film industry's bottomline considerations operated as a form of economic regulatory mechanism.

Rick Paul gave a video copy of *Henry* to Michael Kutza, director of the Chicago International Film Festival, who agreed to show the film. The only problem was that McNaughton did not have a print and the venue for the screening, the Music Box Theatre, did not have video projection. So McNaughton and Rooker hired a video projector and took it to the venue, thus facilitating *Henry*'s first public screening on 24 September 1986. Responses were mixed. Dave Kehr, then critic at the *Chicago Tribune*, gave his video copy of *Henry* to fellow journalist Rick Kogan, who then championed the film in print. McDonough suggests that the screening of *Henry* 'provoked a mixture of admiration and revulsion' (1991, p. 44) whilst James Marriott states that many critics found 'its apparent moral blankness abhorrent' (2004, p. 287). This pattern of reception was to become characteristic of *Henry*'s reviews and helped to stimulate debate by setting up frameworks, which, whilst not determining audience responses, certainly had a bearing on them. After the Chicago Film Festival, screenings of *Henry* continued in late shows at the Music Box Theatre and a few other metropolitan cinemas in the US.

In 1987 a second film based upon the Henry Lee Lucas story was produced. *Confessions of a Serial Killer* (hereafter referred to as *Confessions*) is closer to the biographical details of the Lucas story than *Henry*. Starting with the arrest of Daniel Ray Hawkins (Robert A. Burns – the art director of *The Texas Chainsaw Massacre* (1974), *The Hills Have Eyes* (1977) and *Re-Animator*) the film has him deliver his confessions to the police via a series of flashbacks. Unlike *Henry*, *Confessions* actively seeks to offer an explanation for Hawkins's life of multi-jurisdictional killing by pointing to a range of factors including his abusive upbringing and his itinerant lifestyle. Like *Henry* the film presents its protagonist as unredeemable. *Confessions* was also shelved for several years, eventually being released on video in 1992. Inevitably, it has been largely overshadowed within film history and culture by the furore surrounding *Henry*.

During 1988 Chuck Parello (*Henry: Portrait of a Serial Killer, Part 2* (1998), *In the Light of the Moon* aka *Ed Gein* (2000), *The Hillside Strangler* (2004)) was hired as MPI publicity director. He saw *Henry*, liked it and made it his mission to get the film into theatres. His first move was to send out tapes. As he explains:

> I had been working for MPI for about a year when John and I started to talk about ways to get *Henry* off the shelf. I started showing it to film critics I knew and arranged screenings of it in New York (quoted in McKee, 2008).

He also worked with artist Joe Coleman and his wife to arrange a screening of *Henry* as part of their film festival held in New York. It was here that *Henry* was seen by Elliott Stein, a critic at the *Village Voice*, who wrote an article praising the film; he also placed it in his Top Ten list of 1989. As in the case of *Henry*'s screenings in Chicago, those in New York provoked discussion and controversy, with some judging the film an example of expert film-making and others considering it too unpleasant to watch. The early reception to *Henry* by critics and festival-goers contributed to the crystallizing of the critical discourses circulating around the film and helped to establish the permeable foundations of discussions and controversies to come. During 1989 Coleman created a painting for the movie poster of *Henry* that was later dropped by MPI as too extreme. This was based on the shot of Henry looking at his reflection in a motel bathroom mirror, his face surrounded by images of death and destruction taken from the film and illustrated with lines of dialogue.[12] The image was replaced by a still from the same scene taken by Berndt Rantscheff.

According to McDonough: 'By 1989 *Henry* was sinking into the oblivion of occasional midnight runs in shabby cult theatres, but it wouldn't die' (1991, p. 45). In September 1989 Errol Morris (*The Thin Blue Line* (1988), *The Fog of War* (2003)) brought *Henry* to the Telluride Film Festival in Colorado. McNaughton felt that, along with Michael Moore's *Roger and Me* (1989), *Henry* was the sensation of the festival and it was here that the film had its big break:

> The first time I saw a print projected to an audience was at the Telluride Film Festival. I'd say during the scene where the family is slaughtered, we lost about fifteen percent of the audience. They were flying out the door. But the next screening, when word got around that it was an artistic film, we lost only one person. (Falsetto, 2000, p. 321)

McDonough suggests that *Henry* 'became the talk of the festival' (1991, p. 45) whilst Bouzereau reports that 'audiences, critics and exhibitors were split and shocked by the film' (2000, p. 201). In terms of critical responses, Marriott states that Roger Ebert, who was at the festival, was impressed by the film's 'brutal but honest' tone (2004, p. 287). As far as McNaughton was concerned: 'At this point *Henry* generated enough publicity to qualify as a phenomenon' (2003a, p. 2).

However, if *Henry*'s fortunes were beginning to change, all this attention had not translated into a distribution company offering to pick up and distribute the film theatrically. This demonstrated how the controversy and buzz surrounding *Henry* had not yet tipped the balance sufficiently for it to be considered a commercially viable product in theatrical terms in the US, revealing another overlap between cultural and economic forms of film regulation.

On the strength of *Henry*, McNaughton had been signed for representation by the Gersh Agency in New York. According to McNaughton, after Telluride 'my agent sent me every bad horror-film script that was doing everything we tried so hard not to do in *Henry* ... I couldn't bring myself to do any of them' (Falsetto, 2000, p. 331). However, the unemployed McNaughton eventually agreed to make the sci-fi horror comedy *The Borrower*, financed by

Atlantic Releasing, whose concept he liked but which would turn out to be a horror story of its own both to make and distribute.

US Film Classification

Atlantic Releasing became the second distributor to show an interest in *Henry*. According to McNaughton, after he had signed the deal with Atlantic Releasing to direct *The Borrower*, the company expressed an interest in distributing *Henry* theatrically. The only condition was that *Henry* receive an 'R' rating from the Classification and Rating Administration (CARA) of the Motion Picture Association of America, meaning that children under sixteen would not be admitted to a screening unless accompanied by a parent or adult guardian (the age restriction was later raised to seventeen). However in March 1998, because of the realism, violence and lack of moral judgment on display in *Henry*, the film was awarded an 'X' rating, which meant that no-one under seventeen could be admitted at all. This was one of the few 'X' ratings assigned on the basis of content other than sexually explicit material.

There were several disadvantages to being awarded an 'X' rating, which explain why Atlantic had wanted an 'R'. As the MPAA had no copyright on the 'X' rating, it had been freely appropriated by others, and in particular pornographers, to connote the strength of their films. As such the rating's cultural meaning had shifted from merely 'adult' to 'pornographic' in the American imagination. Consequently many newspapers, radio and TV stations refused to take advertising for 'X' films; most theatre chains would not show them; many mall multiplexes had real-estate contracts prohibiting their exhibition; they could not be broadcast on the majority of TV stations; and were unable fully to exploit the growing video market.

Commenting on this situation, McNaughton remarked: 'I don't have a problem with the rating system itself. Children shouldn't see certain things ... but it shouldn't be penalized in the market place so severely' (quoted in Bouzereau, 2000, p. 201). The treatment of *Henry* reveals the complex ways in which official classification influences, and in turn is influenced by, wider cultural and economic factors. For smaller independent companies like MPI or Atlantic, which cannot afford advertising, the buzz generated by the awarding of an 'X' can bring valuable grassroots publicity and promotion for films that few people would normally even hear about, let alone see. However, Atlantic decided to pull out because it felt that distributing an 'X'-rated film would entail too many financial restrictions.[13] Significantly, whilst *Henry* was produced during the boom in independent film-making of the mid-1980s, it was seeking theatrical distribution during the late 1980s when the sector was feeling the shockwaves of the 1987 US stockmarket crash and a decline in the demand for films.

Around the time of *Henry*'s initial US release, McNaughton reflected that

> normally when you get an 'X' they say: Here are the problems, fix these four scenes. With *Henry*, we never had that option. They couldn't reduce the problems to a few scenes. It was an overall problem. 'Disturbing moral tone' was what they said. What does that mean? (McDonough, 1991, p. 44)

In later commentaries McNaughton has said that he was thankful that the MPAA had not requested cuts, because if they had done so, he would have complied. But as cuts were neither requested nor made, the version eventually released in the US was the director's cut (McNaughton and Gregory, 2005a). In relation to the MPAA decision, Steven Jones stated that:

> People want to cling to the belief that there aren't random acts of violence out there. Well the real Henry went seven years uncaptured. Scary but true. We gave out that message, and it was too emotionally disturbing [for the MPAA]. (McDonough, 1991, p. 44)

Early in 1989 Chuck Parello, on behalf of MPI, which was not an MPAA member, wrote to the MPAA surrendering *Henry*'s 'X' rating. In the henry: portrait of a serial killer   23

US, a film can waive its official MPAA classification and be released unrated, incurring only economic rather than legal sanctions (the situation is very different in the UK, as will become clear later). MPI then decided to sue the MPAA, charging it with discrimination by refusing to grant *Henry* an 'R' rating even though it featured less graphic violence than other 'R'-rated movies. According to McNaughton, 'the frustrating thing is that based upon the MPAA's own standards, *Henry* is an 'R' film. No question about it. But for some reason, applicable standards were not applied' (ibid., p. 44). Waleed B. Ali added to the exasperation, asking:

> What I want to know is how in *Indiana Jones and the Temple of Doom* ... a man sticks his hand into the chest cavity of another man and pulls out a bleeding, beating heart and the movie gets a 'PG' rating? And our movie, which has nothing like that, gets an 'X'? (quoted in Bouzereau, 2000, p. 202)

On 14 May 1990 MPI filed a lawsuit in a federal court in Washington challenging the 'X' rating – another example of a method exploited to raise awareness of and gain publicity for *Henry* that it would not have received without this rating. This case and another – filed by Miramax Films and Pedro Almodóvar contesting the 'X' rating issued to *Tie Me Up! Tie Me Down!* (1990) – were the first suits since 1970 contesting the constitutionality of the MPAA's ratings. Both cases were watched closely by film-makers, who were growing increasingly frustrated by the fact that no rating existed for serious adult films that were not pornographic. At around the time that MPI filed its suit, the MPAA released a statement to the effect that it was confident that the courts would agree with its decision and thus endorse the ratings system as providing a useful system for parents whilst at the same time protecting the creative freedom of film-makers. On 26 September 1990, due in part to the controversy surrounding the challenges to the 'X' ratings given to *Henry*, *Tie Me Up! Tie Me Down!* and also *The Cook, the Thief, His Wife and Her Lover* (1990), the MPAA and the National Association of Theatre Owners announced that they would replace the 'X' with the 'NC-17', which would be given to films to which nobody under seventeen would be admitted. Alongside the 'NC-17' rating, public information on why specific ratings had been given was introduced. However, the 'NC-17' has subsequently been criticized as generating the same problems as the old 'X' rating and further inflamed the deteriorating relationship between the MPAA and its critics. The US District Court for the District of Columbia dismissed the MPI lawsuit in October 1990. On appeal the District Court's decision was overturned, and further proceedings were set for April 1995.

US Theatrical and Video Distribution

Subsequent to being rated 'X', *Henry* was shown at the Boston Film Festival on 14 September 1989, where Greycat Films, a company headed by two former Vestron executives, bought the rights to distribute *Henry* theatrically in the US. An unrated *Henry* had a limited theatrical release, mainly in selected art-house cinemas, in 1990, opening in Boston on 5 January, New York City on 23 March and Los Angeles on 18 April. Those under seventeen are not admitted to unrated films, and the financial disadvantages of releasing a film unrated are similar to those for 'X'-rated films, as theatre chains traditionally do not distinguish between a film with no rating and a film with an 'X'. However, *Henry* had a successful city-by-city release, grossing $609,939 and returning a profit on an investment of $111,000, illustrating how controversy and classification difficulties can actually translate into economic gains, even if these were modest at this stage. Moreover, this limited theatrical release generated a good deal of extra publicity both for the film and McNaughton himself. As a result, *Henry*'s US theatrical career followed a typical independent pattern of limited and platform distribution, which was built upon advanced awareness of the film resulting from festival screenings and prizes, critical reception and reviews, and publicity linked to the award and subsequent surrendering of its 'X' rating.[14]

Henry was released unrated on video by MPI Home Video on 26 September 1990. The packaging for the video featured the text 'TOTALLY UNCUT & UNCENSORED' at the bottom of the frontcover and 'THE MOST CONTROVERSIAL FILM OF THE DECADE' at the top of the rear sleeve. A recurring theme in much of the packaging for *Henry* is this deliberate trading, as a marketing ploy, upon the cultural and classificatory furore associated with the film. The image on the frontcover is a medium close-up shot of Henry staring at his reflection, taken from Berndt Rantscheff's still. The cover also features the line 'HE'S NOT FREDDY, HE'S NOT JASON … HE'S REAL', below which are two quotes from American reviews: 'Two Thumbs Up!' – Siskel and Ebert[15] and '4 Stars. Now This is a Horror Movie!' – Jami Bernard, *New York Post*. The backcover displays the quotes 'A Film of Clutching Terror' – Peter Travers, *Rolling Stone* and 'The Best Film of the Year' – Elliott Stein, *Village Voice*. On 13 November 1991 MPI Home Video released an unrated laserdisc edition of *Henry*. The cover packaging was very similar to the video, the main textual difference being the moving of the Bernard quote to the rearcover and its replacement with the Travers quote from the rearcover of the video release. For low-budget independent films with little or no budget for promotion and advertising, video packaging and film posters are important marketing tools, and frequently attempt to attract audiences by playing up any controversy. However, according to McDonough (1991), *Henry* also felt the economic consequences of Blockbuster Video's self-imposed regulatory policy requiring all franchises to remove unrated films from their shelves.

US Critical Reception

As McDonough notes, the limited release of the unrated *Henry* brought McNaughton 'good press and many new admirers' (1991, p. 45). Similarly Bouzereau (2000) explains, by the time *Henry* had its theatrical run it was already a favourite with many critics, including Jay Carr (*Boston Globe*) and

John M. Glionna (*Los Angeles Times*). Michael Rooker received glowing reviews from critics including Henry Sheehan (*Hollywood Reporter*) and Joe Bob Briggs (*San Francisco Examiner*). As a result, despite delays in its theatrical release, initial reception of *Henry* was characterized by critical acclaim, nominations for several festival awards and placement in a range of top-choice listings. Elliott Stein asserted that *Henry* was 'the best film of the year ... recalls the best work of Cassavetes' (*Village Voice*) and Dave Kehr called it 'one of the ten best films of the year' (*Chicago Tribune*).[16] *Henry* won awards at the 1991 Brussels International Festival of Fantasy Film and at Fantasporto 1991.[17] For Jeffrey Sconce (1993), the critical reputation of *Henry* was formed as much by the cultural context of its release and circulation as it was by its style or vision.

Even though *Henry* was produced during the mid-1980s, it circulated with a number of big-budget 1990s serial-killer films including *Blue Steel* (1990), *The Silence of the Lambs* (1991) and *Kalifornia* (1993); it also coincided with Bret Easton Ellis's novel *American Psycho* and the return of *Twin Peaks* (1991) to US TV. The result in terms of the timing of its distribution was double-edged. On the one hand, the film had had several years in order to build up a buzz but, on the other, its delay meant that it tends to be directly compared to films produced years later. For example, *Henry* is often considered to be at the opposite end of the stylistic spectrum to many of the 'serial killer as superhero' and 'profiler' movies of the 1990s, including *The Silence of the Lambs*[18] and *Se7en* (1995). According to Sconce (1993), this is because *Henry* was deliberately constructed to appeal directly to cinephiles through its use of self-conscious narration, a strategy that enabled critics to gain pleasure from its mode of identification and promote *Henry* as a highbrow alternative to mainstream 'slasher' films such as the *Nightmare on Elm Street* (1984) cycle.

After *Henry's* theatrical release, McNaughton received three high-profile fan letters. One was from John Waters of *Pink Flamingos* (1972) and *Serial Mom* (1994) fame, the second from David Mamet (*House of Games* (1987), *Homicide* (1991)), who would go on to script McNaughton's *Lanksy* and the third from Eric Bogosian. McNaughton met Bogosian in 1991 and agreed to direct the filming of his stage performance *Sex, Drugs, Rock & Roll*. McNaughton was also given his first studio job by Martin Scorsese: as a fan of Scorsese, McNaughton asked his agent to send him a tape of *Henry*. At that point, Scorsese's assistant watched it, hated it and decided not to pass it on. A few years later Melanie Frieson, who worked for Scorsese, saw it, liked it and showed it to him. As a consequence, Scorsese asked McNaughton to read the script for *Mad Dog and Glory* and then hired him to direct it.

This part of the book has examined how the development, pre-production, production and post-production of *Henry* established the foundations upon which the controversy surrounding the film was based, before looking closely at how the dynamic processes of circulation, classification, marketing, advertising and reception within the US context fuelled and fanned that controversy. The next part will examine how the intense debate about *Henry* was influenced by the intersecting roles of censorship, marketing, circulation and reception in the UK. It will also chart the ongoing commodification of *Henry*'s controversy through a successive range of US and UK re-releases.

✖ PART 2

HENRY: PORTRAIT OF A SERIAL KILLER SINCE THEN

Part 2 examines Henry's controversy within the British context, beginning with a study of *Henry*'s struggle with the British Board of Film Classification, initially manifesting in the delayed and censored 1991 theatrical release. This account is augmented with a review of the critical reception of the 1991 theatrical release before moving on to evaluate the further delayed, more heavily censored and also re-edited 1993 video release, the less censored 2001 video release, and the 2003 re-releases of uncut theatrical and DVD versions of the film. There is also an exploration of the ongoing commodification of *Henry* and its controversy through successive US and UK re-releases on DVD, including the 20th Anniversary Special Edition in 2005 and the 2009 Blu-ray release.

UK Film Classification

Henry was submitted to the BBFC by Electric Pictures on 7 January 1990 with a running time of eighty-one minutes and fifty-four seconds (BBFC, 2007). It arrived there at an interesting time; the moral panic over 'video nasties' (1982–4) had subsided (albeit temporarily), but in the wake of the 1987 Hungerford Massacre (which sections of the press had laid at the door of the *Rambo* films, although entirely without foundation), the BBFC had become stricter than ever when it came to the portrayal of weaponry in films. However in the case of theatrical releases, which are not subject to the Video Recordings Act (VRA), which was imposed as a result of the 'nasties' panic, by the mid-1980s, outright bans on films had largely been replaced by the imposition of cuts to fit within age categories. However, this did not mean that films passed in the '18' category were generally let through uncut; as Tom Dewe Mathews argues, because of the 'extraordinary range of conditions imposed by the BBFC on adult-orientated films', 20 per cent of films classified at '18' for theatrical release and home video were cut in order to achieve that rating during 1991 (1994, p. 261).

According to Mark Kermode (2002), *Henry* was originally earmarked for an outright ban. Mathews (1994, p. 263) suggests that when *Henry* arrived at the BBFC, 'everyone on the Board knew that this film would not quietly disappear into a welter of public apathy', as in the case of the controversy over *The Last Temptation of Christ* (1988). *Henry* was voluntarily pre-censored by its distributor Electric Pictures, which removed the third tableau, the cut taking place as Henry drives down a city-centre road and the film resuming with him driving along a freeway. The cut, of thirty-eight seconds, is aurally bridged by the song 'La Lania' but the transition skips a section of the song, thus drawing attention to the cut. As noted earlier, the tableau featured a dead prostitute slumped on a toilet with a broken bottle impaled in her face. This

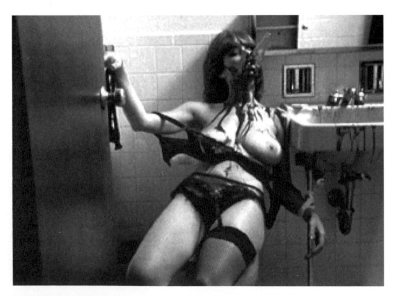

Image from the third tableau that was pre-censored by Electric Pictures.

pre-cutting was carried out to avoid inclining the BBFC to view the film as exploitative, with the aim of trying to ward off more extensive cuts. BBFC Director James Ferman recalled that

> it seemed to me such a prurient, exploitative shot of a female corpse. The sort of thing that I was used to in a very different kind of movie. That scene predisposed me to expect the worst from the rest of it. (quoted in ibid., p. 265)

McNaughton claims he was not consulted about this cut.

Henry was first screened theatrically in the UK without a BBFC certificate at Splatterfest at the Scala Cinema in London's King's Cross in February 1990. The print was an unrated American version that included the third tableau, and several BBFC examiners were present at the screening. It was also screened at the National Film Theatre in London. A disclaimer was added to the beginning of the UK release by the distributor in an attempt to ward off possible legal action. According to McNaughton, lawyers insisted on the disclaimer to avoid relatives filing a lawsuit, and his thoughts were that, as long as it did not appear in the main body of the film he was not concerned.

Henry was not granted an '18' certificate for theatrical release until 24 April 1991 and, according to both Kermode (2002) and Mathews (1994), it came with a promise that it would not receive a video certificate. Mathews outlines how

> *Henry* took more time to censor than almost any other film in modern times and its censorship highlights the BBFC's adoption of the language of psychology and psychiatry as a means to determine who is most liable to be affected by a film.

He argues that it was *Henry*'s 'lack of closure or retribution, along with the film's unrelieved depiction of how arbitrary violence can be, that set the

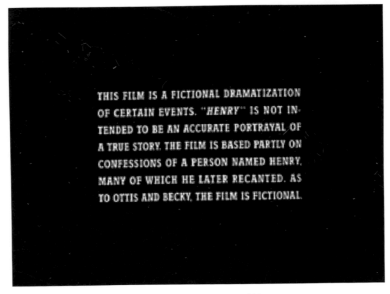

THIS FILM IS A FICTIONAL DRAMATIZATION OF CERTAIN EVENTS. "HENRY" IS NOT IN-TENDED TO BE AN ACCURATE PORTRAYAL OF A TRUE STORY. THE FILM IS BASED PARTLY ON CONFESSIONS OF A PERSON NAMED HENRY, MANY OF WHICH HE LATER RECANTED. AS TO OTTIS AND BECKY, THE FILM IS FICTIONAL.

The disclaimer voluntarily added to the UK versions of *Henry*.

BBFC's alarm bells ringing' (1994, pp. 263–4). Ironically, then, the language of psychology and psychiatry, which in the 1980s had entered factual and fictional discourses around serial killers, and which McNaughton and Fire had deliberately sought to critique in *Henry*, was now directly entering discourse surrounding the censorship of a film about a serial killer.

Ferman wanted to ban *Henry* outright, but he did not have enough support at the BBFC. According to Mathews, one examiner argued that 'no killer wants to look like, live like or be like Henry. On the contrary I think these sort of people want to look like Hannibal Lecter' (quoted in ibid., p. 266). After many screenings and much discussion and argument, the BBFC required twenty-four seconds to be cut from the already self-censored version, amounting to a total of sixty-two seconds of cuts. The BBFC-imposed cuts were taken from the home-invasion scene. For whilst the violent details of the scene, including the breaking of the mother and son's necks, did not pose a problem for the BBFC, what did worry the censors was the way in which the scene had been filmed and edited, as the following extract from an examiner's report illustrates:

> The effect of a film within a film here is not to distance it but rather through the home movie feel, give the impression that this could be located anywhere, including one's own home. Added to that the woman is totally depersonalised. The camera gives us no lead into the assault from her viewpoint and therefore no feel for her as a person. Otis and Henry are already known, however, and, accordingly we see her through their eyes. Conventions from the standard repertoire of filmic sex and violence also operate here, such as the positioning of the woman towards the camera. By these devices viewers are invited to participate, to see the titillatory nature of such cruelty and the film is therefore truly exploitative. (quoted in ibid., p. 265)

Cuts were made to remove the movement of Otis's hand to the murdered wife's pubic area and to reduce to a minimum the mauling of her breasts before and after she is killed (Melon Farmers, 2008). In a further irony, the BBFC removed the very detail encoded into the text by McNaughton that sought to encourage audiences to reflect upon their consumption of violence as entertainment. As mentioned above, the film-makers' express vision within this scene was to present film violence as confrontationally as possible, offering what they saw as a counterbalance to other scenes within the film and horror cinema more generally.

To place the BBFC's treatment of *Henry* within a legal context, in 1977 film in the UK was made subject to the Obscene Publications Act (OPA), although it should be pointed out that nothing passed by the BBFC prior to this point could possibly have been regarded as legally obscene. However, both this and James Ferman's own attitudes made the BBFC very wary of sex scenes, and in particular of scenes involving sexual violence, especially if the violence could in any way be taken to be eroticized. Ferman

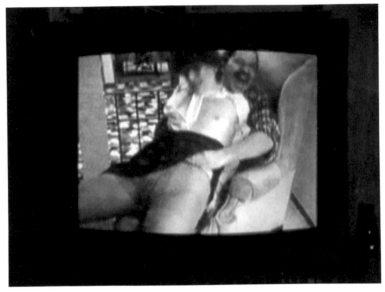

Material cut from the UK cinema version of *Henry* by the BBFC.

in particular felt that the home-invasion scene and the third tableau did indeed contain eroticized sexual violence, and this is why the BBFC censored the former and the distributors saved them the trouble of censoring the latter. The BBFC's initial treatment of *Henry* highlights how the actions of the BBFC are framed by legal requirements (in this case, the OPA); how regulatory power is contested within the BBFC; and how censorship is both voluntary/self-imposed (by the distributor) and mandatory/official (by the BBFC).

    Henry was released theatrically in the UK on 12 July 1991 with a running time of eighty-one minutes and thirty-one seconds. *Screen International* figures report that by 1996 *Henry* had taken £72,598 at the UK box office (Hill, 1997, p. 64). As a result, and as in the US context, *Henry's* theatrical distribution in the UK was modest and limited, with the film playing mostly in a small number of art-house cinemas.

UK Critical Reception of the 1991 Theatrical Release

In their overview of the 1991 reviews of the UK cinema release of *Henry*, Hallam and Marshment (2000) suggest that a discourse of realism was used to either praise or condemn the film. They suggest, similarly to Sconce (1993) in the US, that the reviews reveal more about the intellectual tastes and preferences of the writer than they do about the film. Reviewers such as Adam Mars-Jones in the *Independent* dismissed the film as deeply disturbing due to the fact that its semi-documentary realist form 'cheats' the audience by presenting no explanation for Henry's actions (Hallam and Marshment, 2000, p. 236). Other reviewers were more concerned about the underlying ideological meanings within *Henry*. Thus Amy Taubin complains apropos the home-invasion scene that 'a film that started off being about psychopathology and its relationship to misogyny has turned blatantly misogynist' (1991, p. 17). However, Hallam and Marshment hold that, on balance, the reviews were supportive of the film and its realism. Several reviewers suggested that *Henry* offered a necessary corrective to films such as *The Silence of the Lambs*; for example, Alexander Walker in the *Evening Standard* argued that 'many films feature violent death but they dramatise it – all *Henry* does is record it' (quoted in Hallam and Marshment, 2000, p. 236). Kim Newman also takes this approach, noting that 'unlike the Thomas Harris-derived films and other entries in the serial-killer cycle – *Henry* has no interest whatsoever in the cocktail of issues that surround the killings' (1991, p. 44). What the reviews as a whole tend to reveal is that for some reviewers the lack of moral perspective in *Henry* was a real problem, whereas for others this was a positive feature of the film. A number of reviews also demonstrate how, as noted earlier, in the UK *Henry* was compared with films produced several years later, because of the gap between its production and release. Issues linked to realism and authenticity will be discussed in the following chapter.

UK 1993 Video Release

As previously mentioned, when *Henry* was released theatrically, BBFC
Director James Ferman told Electric Pictures that it would not receive a video
certificate in the UK. Such pronouncements by Ferman can be viewed as an
informal mechanism employed by the BBFC to manage the types of film
violence, and the number of controversial films, entering the public domain at
this time. However, the BBFC, somewhat surprisingly, did not come under fire
for passing *Henry* (albeit in cut form) for the cinema. As a consequence, and
encouraged by its largely positive critical reception in the UK, Electric decided
to persist with plans for a video release in the UK – it was already available on
video in continental Europe and the US – and they submitted it to the BBFC
for video classification in the latter half of 1991. The Video Recordings Act
1984 enshrined in law the BBFC's statutory responsibility to assign special
regard to the likelihood of video works being viewed in the home, and the
BBFC has traditionally taken this to mean that it has at least to consider the
possibility that any certificated video may be seen by children. It also takes into
account that, on video, scenes can be freeze-framed, viewed in slow motion or
watched over and over again, activities which it feels could be harmful in
certain cases. Consequently, there can be a major disparity between the BBFC's
treatment of cinema and video versions of films. This was certainly the case
with *Henry*. Indeed, Ferman explicitly raised the nature of the video-viewing
experience when explaining his reasons for cutting the video of Henry:

> We were worried about the small proportion of viewers who would use
> the family murder scene to feed their own fantasies because on video
> you can control your fantasies, play scenes over and over again, just as
> Henry and Otis are controlling their own fantasies when they are re-living
> the killings on video. (quoted in Kermode, 1995, p. 42)

During the censoring of the UK video version of *Henry*, the BBFC
drew upon the evidence of two psychiatrists whom they consulted about the

possible effects of the film. According to Mathews, the psychiatrists felt that 'the playback capacity of video could be employed by murderers to endlessly rehearse a killing; and, once primed, the potential killers would be ready to go out and "do the real thing"' (1994, p. 266). Mathews also cites BBFC Deputy Director Margaret Ford as claiming that the psychiatrists reported that the murders in *Henry* could indeed 'disinhibit the guys with eggshell skulls, the ones who you don't have to go very far to arrive at their psyches' (ibid.). Mathews argues that the views of the psychiatrists vindicated Ferman's belief that a film's fantasy gradually becomes reality for 'potential criminals' (ibid.). Thus, according to Ferman:

> All the material we cut [from *Henry*] was violence connected with sexual abuse of a victim. Therefore it could have got past the guard of the audience. Once you're into sexual images you can turn people on because whatever one part of their mind is telling them, another part is telling them something else. (quoted in ibid.)

In Mathews's view, the censorship of *Henry* 'supposedly acted both to remove the "disinhibitors" which affect those people "the Board is most worried about", and also to put a stop to anyone else's involuntary sexual arousal at the sight of rape' (ibid.). Viewed thus, the home-invasion scene can be seen as representing the BBFC's very worst fears about the potential harm to audiences and, through their resultant behaviour, to society as a whole, through watching sexualized film violence.

The BBFC eventually classified the video version of *Henry* on 26 January 1993 with one minute fifty-three seconds of cuts and a running time of seventy-seven minutes twenty-six seconds (BBFC, 2007). The BBFC maintained the cuts from the cinema version and required an additional fifty-one seconds of cuts. Here it is important to note the contrasting approaches to *Henry* by the MPAA and the BBFC for, whereas the MPAA did not specify what should be removed, simply indicating that the film's 'moral tone' which made it an 'X', in the UK the BBFC singled out specific cuts from certain

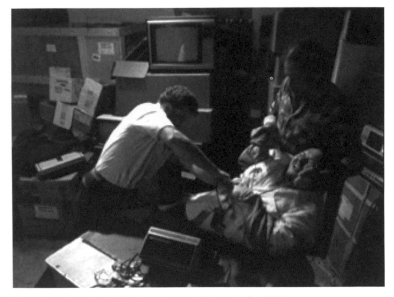

Material cut from the 1993 video release of *Henry* by the BBFC.

scenes in order to remove potentially harmful material and enable the film to
be awarded an '18' certificate. Thus four seconds of cuts were required to the
'shopping' scene to reduce the number of times the fence is stabbed with a
soldering iron (Melon Farmers, 2008). The violence here was presumably
thought to be 'excessive'.

Further, and more significant, cuts were required to the home-invasion
scene. In addition to the twenty-four seconds removed from the theatrical
version, the video version was trimmed by a further forty-seven seconds to
remove the violent detail of the killing of the mother and son. Ferman stated
that: 'The principle we followed in cutting the scene was to cut out the
masturbatory pleasure. We were worried about the sexual turn-on element for
solitary men watching at home' (quoted in Mathews, 1994, p. 268). In total the
BBFC required one minute eleven seconds of cuts from the UK video version of
this scene, which lasts four minutes nine seconds in total. There are four main

cuts: the first takes place after the mother's bra is pulled over her breast, and cut footage includes Otis squeezing her left breast before lifting her skirt and putting his hand down the front of her tights whilst Henry offers encouragement. The second cut takes place after Henry repeatedly kicks the father and resumes just before the son enters the room. The cut footage involves detail of Otis struggling with the mother and kissing one of her breasts whilst behind the camera Henry shouts support. The third cut removes violent detail of the struggle between Henry and the son and the breaking of both the son's and mother's necks. The fourth cut takes place after Henry stabs the father off screen and Otis starts kissing the dead mother. The scene resumes as Otis is preparing to remove her tights. Removed footage includes Henry picking up the camera and surveying the dead, and Otis molesting the dead mother.

Drastic as they were, it seemed that these cuts alone were not enough for Ferman; he was still worried about the possible effects of the home-invasion

Material cut by the BBFC from the 1993 video version of the home-invasion scene.

scene on audiences. The scene was thus *re-edited* to move a reaction shot of Henry and Otis watching their homemade 'snuff movie' from the end of the scene to a much earlier point in it. The re-edit takes place approximately thirty-two seconds into the invasion and the shot lasts around five seconds. The re-edit served, in combination with the third cut listed above, to replace images of the murder of the son and mother. This re-editing, according to Mathews (1994), was an attempt not so much to prevent psychopathic behaviour as interrupt any 'masturbatory potential' that Ferman felt the scene contained. Mathews rightly noted that the act of adding to, as well as subtracting from, *Henry*, completely overstepped the role of regulator; furthermore, it undermined the very moment in the film at which audiences are implicated in the actions of Henry and Otis. *Time Out* critic Nigel Floyd noted that 'by pre-empting the crucial moment at which our guilty complicity is exposed, Ferman's version subverts this moment of subversion' (quoted in ibid., p. 268): Mark Kermode agreed:

> What was most distressing about the BBFC's tampering with *Henry* was that not only did Ferman choose to cut McNaughton's vision, he also surreptitiously re-edited it, quite deliberately, to change the very meaning of the film. ... The result, as ever, was to deface and defile a radical work of art, to make it 'palatable' in a way which utterly negated its entire *raison d'être*. (2002, p. 19)

And McNaughton himself stated that 'to rearrange that scene is to relieve the audience of the responsibility that is intended to be built into the scene' (2003c).

The first video version of *Henry* was released into the UK rental market during March 1993 and the UK retail market in January 1994. Around this time a laserdisc of *Henry* was released in the UK by Encore Entertainment.[19] Contextually this is significant because the controversy surrounding *Henry*'s first cut UK video release coincided with a renewal of the moral panic over 'video nasties'. On 12 February 1993, two-year-old James Bulger was

The reaction shot which Ferman re-edited so as to feature it earlier
in the home-invasion scene in the cut 1993 UK video release.

abducted, tortured and killed by two ten-year-olds, Robert Thompson and Jon
Venables. Thompson and Venables were tried in November 1993 amidst lurid
(and entirely untrue) stories about the boys having been influenced by horror
videos, and notably by *Child's Play 3* (1993), prompting a concerted campaign
by the Movement for Christian Democracy, the Liberal Democrat MP David
Alton, various child specialists and sections of the press, to demand yet tighter
regulation of films on video. This 'second episode' of the 'nasties' panic resulted
in an amendment being made to the VRA by the Criminal Justice and
Public Order Act during April 1994. This required the BBFC to take into
account the 'harm' that certain kinds of video images, namely those depicting
criminal behaviour, the use of illegal drugs, violent behaviour or incidents,
horrific behaviour or incidents and human sexual activity, might do to those
who viewed them, and, through their subsequent behaviour, any harm which

might be done to society as a whole. (For a series of accounts of this episode, see Barker, 1997). Whilst *Henry* was already circulating on video during this period, it is interesting to speculate what might have happened to it had it been submitted to the BBFC in the immediate post-Bulger period, in which numerous horror films fell victim to the newly empowered BBFC.

The packaging for the 1994 sell-through UK video release contained a warning banner in the top lefthand corner, 'WARNING: THIS FILM CONTAINS SCENES WHICH MAY BE DISTURBING TO SOME VIEWERS'. It is important to note that the inclusion of this prominent warning was not a requirement of the BBFC. Rather, the warning served as another exploitational marketing technique deployed to attract audiences by foregrounding the film's controversial content. The frontcover features the review quote, 'An outstandingly good film ... everyone who saw *The Silence of the Lambs* should see *Henry*' – Alexander Walker, the *Standard*. The back of the video cover presents three more UK review quotes: 'A bold, brave and brilliant film' – *Blast*; 'The most overwhelmingly powerful film I've ever seen. A grim masterpiece' – *Daily Express*; and 'Brilliant, Believable ... An American Masterwork' – *Financial Times*. Thus the marketing of *Henry* clearly drew directly on its perceived extreme, controversial and disturbing content.

US Director's Edition 1998

On 3 November 1998, MPI Home Video released an unrated Region 1 Director's Edition of *Henry*. The cover of the DVD was based on the 1990 MPI video release, the main addition being the inclusion of the words 'DIRECTOR'S EDITION' within a yellow banner at the top of the frontcover, drawing attention to itself against the dark background of the box. The only additions present on the DVD release comprised a short interview with McNaughton and a number of informational bullet points about the film and its cast labelled as 'Factoids', 'Behind the Scenes: Notes' and

'Filmographies'. This release marked a shift in the marketing of *Henry*, signalling a new phase in the exploitation and commodification of the film,[20] building upon its growing status, attracting new audiences, encouraging fans to reinvest in a new edition and capitalizing on the release of the sequel. More generally, the release of the Director's Edition marked a wider recognition during the later 1990s that DVD provided the opportunity to produce and distribute a range of extras likely to appeal to audiences interested in American independent films such as *Henry*.

On 14 August 1998 *Henry: Portrait of a Serial Killer, Part 2* (1996) (hereafter *Henry 2*) was released in the US. The film was written and directed by Chuck Parello, who worked for MPI. He had pushed hard to obtain a cinematic release for *Henry*, and had been an assistant to McNaughton on *Mad Dog and Glory* and *Normal Life*. The film was produced by MPI. McNaughton was not directly involved with the project as he felt his career had moved on and he did not want to return to old material. However, Parello (2002) suggests that McNaughton 'grandfathered' the project by looking at the script and then a cut of *Henry 2*. Henry was played by Neil Giuntoli (*Child's Play* (1988), *The Borrower*, *The Shawshank Redemption* (1994)). Several of the crew of *Henry* returned to work on *Henry 2*, including Waleed B. Ali (producer), Robert McNaughton (composer), Rick Paul (production designer) and Patricia Hart (wardrobe). In the film, a homeless Henry is taken in by a co-worker, Kai (Rich Komenich) and his family. Kai is a part-time arsonist who instructs Henry in his trade in exchange for lessons in how to kill. Louisa (Carri Levinson), a niece who lives with Kai and Cricket (Kate Walsh), his wife, fall for Henry.[21] The tensions build up between Kai, Louisa and Cricket until Henry kills them and burns down their house before moving on once more. Parello (2002) suggests that, whilst *Henry 2* is an homage to its predecessor, it was nonetheless made in its own way. The film received an 'R' rating for its gruesome murders, additional violence, as well as sex, bad language and drug use. At the time, Parello (2002) suggested that he could not rule out the possibility of *Henry 3* because of the track record and financial success of the *Henry* brand. In respect of branding, it is significant that in European countries such as Germany and the Netherlands the two *Henry* films were released together on DVD as a special edition.

UK 2001 DVD Release

On 20 April 2001 the BBFC classified the video and DVD of *Henry* at '18' with cuts. The 2001 release had been submitted by Universal Pictures (UK) Limited to the BBFC with a running time of seventy-nine minutes and fifteen seconds. On this occasion the film was cut by forty-eight seconds (ten seconds of the home-invasion scene by the BBFC and thirty-eight seconds of the third tableau by Universal). These cuts gave the release a running time of seventy-eight minutes twenty-seven seconds. Once again the BBFC required cuts to remove images of sexual violence in line with the Board's policy on this issue (BBFC, 2007). By now the BBFC was including consumer advice on DVD and video boxes, and the text for *Henry* read: 'Language: Some, coarse. Sex/Nudity: Infrequent, strong. Violence: Frequent, strong, bloody. Other: None.'

  The four-second cut made to the murder of the fence during the 'shopping' scene in the 1993 video release was waived. Most of the cuts made to the home-invasion scene in the 1993 video release were also waived (ibid.), although ten seconds of this were cut to remove the sexualized image of the mother's breasts being mauled. Analysis of this release reveals that the cut is approximately the same as the first cut in the 1993 UK video version, although it starts slightly earlier – the pulling up of the mother's bra included in the 1993 version is missing here. The scene resumes with a cut to the husband lying on the floor. All post-mortem sexual abuse and humiliation of the mother is left intact in this version. In all, sixty-one seconds of cuts made to the 1993 video version of *Henry* were waived for the 2001 video and DVD releases. Ferman's re-editing of the home-invasion scene was also removed. As Mark Kermode states, 'The subsequent undoing of Ferman's re-editing jinx by his successors in 2001 merely confirms how muddle-headed his actions were in the first place' (2002, p. 19). According to the cover notes on the 2001 DVD release: 'The director's original intention has therefore now been revealed with minimum intervention from the BBFC to remove erotic potential.'

The BBFC requested seventeen seconds of cuts from the third tableau featuring a dead prostitute with a broken bottle impaled in her face. The Board agreed that the beginning of the scene could be left in, showing the camera panning across the motel room to reveal the dead prostitute on the toilet, but cuts were required to the zoom into and pan up the woman's bloodstained body[22] (Melon Farmers, 2008). However, Universal chose to remove the whole tableau rather than cut the scene as directed, as it felt that this would have looked too clumsy. As noted earlier, the tableau had already been removed in its entirety by the film's then UK distributor, Electric Video, from the 1991 cinema and 1993 video versions. This demonstrates the articulation between official, voluntary and economic forms of film censorship, in that Electric pre-censored the tableau in an effort to placate James Ferman, whilst Universal cut it out in order not to make it obvious that the scene had been censored (knowledge of which might put off potential buyers of the video/DVD). Thus Electric may have, and Universal certainly did, cut out more than had been officially required.

The 2001 video and DVD release was thus the most complete version of the film to be classified in the UK theatrically or on home video up to that point.[23] The DVD packaging, which was different from the 1993 Electric Pictures release, took full advantage of this fact with the heading 'INCLUDES FOOTAGE PREVIOUSLY UNSEEN IN THE UK', whilst also noting that this was 'THE MOST COMPLETE VERSION RELEASED TO DATE IN THE UK'. The package also carried the words: 'WARNING: THIS FILM CONTAINS SCENES WHICH MAY BE DISTURBING TO SOME VIEWERS', printed in yellow at the top of the frontcover in order to make it stand out. The main image on the frontcover is a grainy medium shot of Henry staring at his reflection in the motel mirror.

The bottom of the frontcover presents two quotes from reviewers: 'A film of ferocious power' – *Time Out* and 'The most overwhelmingly powerful film I have ever seen. A masterpiece' – *Daily Express*. Sleevenotes accompanying the release offered an historical account of the film's circulation, reception and regulatory history in the UK. These represent yet more examples of distributors capitalizing on the controversy and censorship history of *Henry* in an attempt to attract new audiences.

The 2001 re-release of Henry in a less heavily cut version reveals several interesting contextual changes in official UK film regulation around this time. In 1998 Ferman retired, precipitating a change in management style at the BBFC. The organization became more open as evidenced in 2000 by the first-ever publication of classification guidelines, based in part upon public consultation. Some believed that the Board was undergoing a period of liberalization. By this time, memories of the second episode of the video-nasty panic had faded, and this created an environment in which several previously banned and controversial films began to be released in either cut or uncut versions on home video. However, the BBFC was still bound by the terms of the amended Video Recordings Act, which at least partly explains why it still felt it necessary to cut *Henry*, albeit less drastically than on previous occasions.

UK 2003 DVD and Theatrical Releases

On 20 February 2003 the BBFC finally passed *Henry* uncut at '18' for theatrical re-release (BBFC, 2007). It had been submitted to the Board by its new UK distributor, Optimum Releasing, with a running time of eighty-two minutes thirty-one seconds. No cuts were made by the distributor prior to submission. The theatrical re-release was accompanied by the consumer advice that the film 'contains strong language and horror'. *Henry* was re-released in UK cinemas on 2 May 2003, marking the first time that *Henry* had been distributed and exhibited uncut theatrically in the UK, outside of festivals, since the original screenings of *Henry* at Splatterfest and the National Film Theatre during the early 1990s.

On 19 March 2003 the BBFC passed *Henry* uncut at '18' on DVD for distribution by Optimum Releasing. The contents of the DVD were exactly the same as in the theatrical release, although the DVD had a running time of seventy-nine minutes fifteen seconds on account of PAL speed-up (ibid.). The theatrical re-release was accompanied by the consumer advice: 'Language: Some, strong. Sex/Nudity: Some, strong. Violence: Frequent, sexual, strong. Other: None' (ibid.). It is interesting to note the more detailed consumer advice offered on the DVD release compared to the theatrical version, a clear indication of the way in which home and cinema entertainment are viewed differently from one another by the BBFC. The uncut DVD was released in the UK on 26 May 2003. The DVD release was accompanied by a range of extras, including a commentary, and its packaging was different again from the 1993 and 2001 versions, taking full advantage of the film's change in regulatory status in the UK. The words 'THE FULL UNCUT VERSION' feature prominently in black letters in a silver banner at the top of the box. Towards the bottom of the frontcover is the line 'He's not Freddy. He's not Jason. He's Real', a statement which, as already noted, originally featured on the original 1990 MPI video and laserdisc releases of *Henry* in America but which is missing from the 1998 Director's Edition. The main image on the frontcover is a medium close-up of Henry staring at his reflection in the motel mirror from a reverse angle to the US MPI releases, and presented underneath the word 'HENRY'. The image is red and black, the letters of the title laid over the image are bordered in white, and the cover itself is black. The rearcover features three review quotes, and one from the film: 'Wrenchingly violent ... A scary and scarring experience'– *Time Magazine*; 'A film full of ferocious, haunting power'– *Time Out*; 'As fine a film as it is a brutally disturbing experience'– *LA Times*; and the line of dialogue 'Yeah, I killed my Mama ...'. Up to this point, the review quotes used on the film's packaging in both the US and the UK had been territory-specific, but this release blended US and UK reviews.

US 20th Anniversary Special Edition and Blu-ray Releases

On 27 September 2005 Dark Sky Films, a trademark of the MPI Media Group, released an unrated, two-disc, all-regions 20th Anniversary Special Edition of *Henry*. This version was different from the Director's Edition in that it offered a range of extras. The packaging also differed from previous editions, offering a reversible cover. The frontcover sports the review quote 'One of the 20 scariest movies of all time' – *Entertainment Weekly*, whilst the back features the review quote 'Now this is a horror movie' – *New York Post*, which had appeared on the frontcovers of the original 1990 video release and the 1998 Director's Edition. Interestingly, the frontcover for this release, whilst based upon the original still taken by Berndt Rantscheff, in which Henry gazes at his own reflection in a motel mirror, which was used on the majority of other promotional material, presents two images of Henry's reflection looking out of the cover. The text on the reverse cover is the same but features the controversial poster artwork designed by Joe Coleman, which had been banned from the original release of *Henry*. The reverse cover also carries different production stills from the frontcover.

With increasing penetration of the market by the Blu-ray format towards the end of the decade, Dark Sky Films prepared an unrated, region A, Blu-ray edition of *Henry*, which was released on 29 September 2009. The release shares many of the extras available on the 20th anniversary release, including a commentary, a 'making of' documentary (*Portrait: The Making of Henry*), a Henry Lee Lucas documentary, deleted scenes, a stills gallery and original storyboards. Once again this Blu-ray release, along with the 20th Anniversary Special Edition, demonstrates the ongoing commodification of *Henry*, exploiting the film's controversial history and growing cult status.

This chapter has focused on the critical reception of *Henry* in the UK and provided a history of its classification and censorship by the BBFC. Apart from being important to an understanding of how the controversy surrounding *Henry* was used to sell the film, its classification history also charts the interesting relationship between film, regulation and fears about crime in the UK. First, it demonstrates the shifting nature of the boundaries governing what are regarded as legally acceptable representations of sexual violence and criminality in films, as institutionalized through laws such as the Video Recordings Act and the regulatory policies and practices of the BBFC. And second, it shows how the VRA requires the BBFC actually to attempt to help prevent sexual violence and criminal behaviour within society through the regulation, censorship and classification of home video.[24]

Having focused on the impact that production, circulation and regulation had upon the controversy surrounding *Henry* in America and the UK, the next part will examine some of the film's key themes. A range of overlapping issues, ideas and debates linked to context, text and audiences will be explored in order to help to explain this controversy.

✖ PART 3

KEY THEMES AND IDEAS

This section takes a range of key themes and evaluates how they contribute to the understanding of what provoked and sustained the controversy surrounding *Henry*. Building upon the position outlined in the Introduction, namely that *Henry* is structurally and stylistically an 'exercise in purposeful confusion' and 'instability' (Rubin, 1992, pp. 54–7), it will be argued that a number of intersecting factors have contributed to *Henry* being so controversial, for so long and in a number of countries. The key ideas, themes and debates are organized into three broad, complementary sections: context – overlapping contexts, film violence and the serial-killer subgenre; text – narrative, form and debates linked to realism and authenticity; and audience – viewers' emotional responses to the fictional violence in *Henry*. In the course of this part of the book, it will be suggested that *Henry* has remained controversial precisely because it engages directly and provocatively with a number of social, cultural and political fissures; that it works within and against Hollywood's generic, narrative and formal codes, conventions and thematic preoccupations; and that it has the potential to test audiences' thresholds and boundaries in relation to the consumption of film violence. The line of argument builds upon subjects explored elsewhere in the book, including the film's production and distribution, its censorship and classification, the cultural politics of its critical reception, and its influence as perceived by the UK regulators. It also sets up discussions that will be developed in later sections, for example around form, narrative and film violence and issues linked to the film's generic and cultural legacy (Part 5).

Context

One of the key reasons why *Henry* was so contentious was because of the shifting and overlapping social, political, economic, industrial and aesthetic contexts within which it was produced, circulated and consumed. Every era has its collective and individual nightmares, and *Henry* was not only a powerful reimagining of some of these fears but also challenged them without providing any comfortable or easy answers (Rubin, 1992; Pence, 1994; Simpson, 2000; Hantke, 2001). The debate engendered by *Henry* should not be seen as unique, however; rather, it ought to be understood in relation to other controversies and, culturally, as embedded within a history of concerns about the relationship between film and society (Kuhn, 1988; Murdock, 1997; Petley, 1997). For Julian Petley, a theme running throughout British cultural history has been the process of linking social and political fears to popular cultural forms. The outcome of this process, according to Graham Murdock, is the formation of 'reservoirs of dogma', symbolic lagoons of social fears and negative stereotypes relating to the impact of popular cultural forms upon their audiences (1997, p. 67). Consequently, the controversy over *Henry* needs to be seen as being located within this broader cultural formation and as having contributed to the symbolic topping-up of these reservoirs over the past three decades.

   Henry was born out of a social and political context of heightened awareness about real violence and mediated real violence in the US, including TV coverage of the Vietnam War, urban race riots, the assassinations of the Kennedys and Martin Luther King, and political demonstrations and their suppression (Rubin, 1992; Cettl, 2003). One of the cultural manifestations of these social and political upheavals was the influence that they had on the representation of film violence in the US. Prince (2000) cites 1967 as a watershed moment, suggesting that changes in the look of film violence were influenced by two main aesthetic shifts: in film form (multi-camera filming, rapid editing, close-ups and slow motion); and in special effects, which increasingly focused upon graphic imagery of bodily mutilation (blood, squibs and prosthetics). For Prince, these factors have increasingly combined to stylize film violence and to increase its potential to provoke controversial responses from audiences, reviewers and regulators. Key examples from this period include *Bonnie and Clyde* (1967), *The Wild Bunch* (1969), *Night of the*

Living Dead (1968) and *A Clockwork Orange* (1971). These shifts in the filmic representation of violence were also made possible by the replacement of the Production Code with the new rating system in 1968. This situation helped to tip the balance in film, from an emphasis on narrative (realism, linearity, actions based on cause and effect) towards spectacle (formalism, spectacular moments and violent shocks) (Charney, 2001).

Historically, whilst *Henry* entered into this social, political, cultural, aesthetic and institutional mix further down the line, it did so echoing and challenging ideas, discourses and concerns that had been circulating within the US for some time. For example, *Henry* evoked social fears of random stranger violence and serial killing, while challenging FBI criminological profiling, behavioural psychological explanations and law-enforcement paradigms for dealing with serial killers. It also responded to increased news media focus on serial killers; engaged with raised public and subcultural interest in real serial killers; and entered into fictional and popular cultural engagement with the phenomenon in film, TV and literature (Pence, 1994; Simpson, 2000). *Henry* was controversial precisely because of its challenging engagement with and reimagining of these increasingly acute anxieties, particularly fears about rising levels of both real and cinematic violence, which, paradoxically, seemed index-linked to a growing interest in the serial-killer phenomenon.

During the 1980s and 1990s the US and UK adopted a more right-wing and neo-conservative agenda under the leaderships of Ronald Reagan (1981–9), George Bush (1989–93), Margaret Thatcher (1979–90) and John Major (1990–7).[25] In both nations there were calls for a return to 'traditional' family values and growing opposition to forms of culture perceived as overly liberal. These often clustered around cultural concerns about the negative effects of violence in the media, especially in films, taking the form of moral panics; demands for stronger censorship in order to protect children and other 'vulnerable' groups; and the 'othering' of audience groups who chose to watch films regarded by the moralists as too violent (Cohen, 2002; Barker, 1995; Kimber, 2000). In the UK, as already noted, moral panics over the alleged effects of film violence were prompted by the circulation of the so-called 'video nasties' in the early 1980s and reignited by the massacres at Hungerford (1987) and Dunblane (1996), and the murder of James Bulger (1993). In the US there were similar concerns linked to school shootings and civil unrest (Hallam and Marshment, 2000). Moral panics can be regarded as cultural forms of regulation, which, in this case, not only helped to fuel debate around a wide range of films, including *Henry*, but also contributed to their stringent official regulation, censorship and classification in the US, UK and other countries, as noted earlier.

One outcome of this situation was that popular culture developed into the site of an ideological battleground fought over between the New Right and Left Liberals in what Lyons (1997) calls the 'Culture Wars'. *Henry* appeared right in the middle of this battlefield. Significantly in this context, as outlined in previous chapters, *Henry* was produced outside the Hollywood system; engaged formally and thematically with the darker side of video technologies' private, domestic usage; and played a part in the challenge to and eventual replacement of the 'X' rating by the 'NC-17' in the US, whilst in the UK it was cut and recut by the BBFC in accordance with the amended Video Recordings Act.

Examination of the political, economic and cultural contexts of the US and UK during the 1980s and 1990s reveals five overlapping aspects of the furore surrounding *Henry*. First, it did not occur in a vacuum but, rather, was very much a product of its time and place within specific national and transnational political and cultural struggles.

Second, it reveals an articulation between official, cultural, economic and self-imposed forms of film regulation, censorship and classification, which manifested itself in a number of outcomes over time and in a range of places. For example, in a trope that will be familiar to those cognizant of cult films and their audiences, the BBFC's censorship decisions spurred in some a desire to see an uncut version of *Henry*, whilst other audiences were led to avoid the film altogether.

Third, it illustrates the complex, fluid and contested operations of regulatory power within a given place over time and within a range of intersecting political, cultural, institutional and economic contexts. Fourth, it shows the ways in which a host of meanings have been built up around *Henry* as a result of the debates in which it has been involved, and how these then frame future responses to the film. And finally, it reveals social fears and concerns over film violence on the cultural, economic, political and institutional levels (Hendershot, 1998). Given these circumstances, controversy was almost inevitable.

Whilst *Henry* was produced during the 1980s, emerging out of and in response to a particular set of contexts and concerns, it did not achieve mainstream distribution and exhibition until the early 1990s, thus locating it within a revised set of circumstances and contexts. As Newman argues:

> The four-year delay between the 1985 conception of *Henry* and its American release, with a further two years between that and its appearance in Britain, means that the movie has run the risk of coming out long after the *cognoscenti* have elected it to cult status and the creative personnel have joined, albeit ambiguously, the mainstream. (1991, p. 44)

Putting to one side for a moment the cultural implications of this quotation, this hiatus between production and distribution is another important contextual factor in the potency and longevity of the disputes surrounding *Henry*. This is because *Henry* was slightly out of place during the early 1990s, making it even more difficult for audiences to pin down their responses to it. If *Henry* was, as has already been suggested, a formal exercise in 'purposeful confusion' and 'instability' (Rubin, 1992), then the gap between its production and mainstream release in both the US and UK only compounded the situation. Moreover, as Newman points out, this situation was augmented by the hype that had circulated around *Henry* during the hiatus.

To illustrate how *Henry* was somewhat out of place upon its eventual mainstream release and how this impacted upon the controversy attached to the film, it would be useful to undertake a brief contextual evaluation of

American film violence during the 1980s and 1990s. The 1980s was a decade where mainstream American film violence was characterized by hypermasculine cartoon-action violence (*First Blood* (1982), *Commando* (1985)) and SFX-driven slasher movies (*Friday the 13th* (1980), *A Nightmare on Elm Street* (1984)). A staple ingredient of film violence since the 1970s, and particularly in the 1980s, has been sexual violence against women – for example, *I Spit on Your Grave* (1978) and *Dressed to Kill* (1980). According to Andrew Male, 'By the '80s, storylines had been stripped down to the point where they were little more than a state-of-the-art delivery system designed to take the maximum impact of excess and violence to the screen' (1997, pp. 32–3). As outlined in Part 1, McNaughton and Fire's vision for *Henry* was to offer a counterbalance to Hollywood's action violence, removing the buffer of fantasy that they felt existed in much horror at the time. However, they have also been criticized for tapping into and reflecting these trends in American film violence rather than challenging them in any significant way (Taubin, 1991; McKinney, 1993; Carter and Weaver, 2003). For Male, the depiction of violence in film during the 1990s was no longer a coherent entity with any fixed meaning, and he points to a fragmentation in the representation of film violence into, for example, the cold and dispassionate *Henry*, the choreographed excess of movement, spectacle, colour and noise in John Woo movies and violent comedies about film violence such as *C'est arrivé près de chez vous/Man Bites Dog* (1991) and *Scream* (1996) (1997, p. 33).

Having said this, a dominant theme of American film violence during the 1990s has been described as a 'new wave' of extremely violent films, what Carter and Weaver (2003) refer to as 'designer violence' and Hill (1997) as 'new brutalism'. According to Hill (1997, p. 11), 'new brutalism' refers to a number of uncompromising films which focus upon individual rather than state violence and which employ a realist aesthetic when representing violence. Films in this category include *Reservoir Dogs* (1992), *Bad Lieutenant* (1992), *Man Bites Dog*, *True Romance* (1993), *Pulp Fiction* (1994), *Killing Zoe* (1994) and, of course, *Henry*. Hallam and Marshment (2000) argue that the use of realist codes and conventions within these films helped to make them contentious and central to debates about realism in cinema. Such codes and conventions included adopting filming techniques generally associated with documentary film-making, utilizing looser narrative structures and employing a style of narration that is often expositional rather than classical. Issues linked to realism are also explored in the next chapter.

A further trend within American film violence during the 1990s was the success of mainstream serial-killer films such as *The Silence of the Lambs*, *Natural Born Killers* (1994) and *Se7en*. The hiatus between the production and mainstream circulation of *Henry*, coupled with the shifting meanings surrounding film violence during the 1980s and 1990s, including the emphasis placed upon violent spectacle, and the provocative expositional nature of McNaughton and Fire's vision, helped to fuel controversy across shifting aesthetic, temporal and spatial contexts.

Henry has been variously categorised as a 'serial killer film' (Simpson, 2000; Cettl, 2003; Marriott, 2004), 'horror film' (Marriott and Newman, 2006), 'slasher film' (Armstrong, 2003), 'crime film' (Hardy, 1997), and an example of 'exploitation cinema' (Tudor, 1989) or 'psycho killer' or 'psycho cinema' (Rubin, 1992; Fuchs, 2002). It has also been cited as an example of 'realist horror' (Freeland, 1995), 'post-modern horror' (Pinedo, 1997; Freeland, 1995) and as intersecting the 'horror genre and the psycho-realism of independent cinema' (Pence, 1994). *Henry* has been further described as exhibiting 'strong violence' (McKinney, 1993), 'designer violence' (Carter and Weaver, 2003) and, as noted above, 'new brutalism' (Hill, 1997; Hallam and Marshment, 2000). McNaughton adds to the mix when he states that *Henry* is a character study, not a serial-killer film or horror film, and that it blends horror and art: '*Henry* stylistically took some of the gore effects and stuff from B-movies, from horror films, but we also took from Cassavetes. It's an amalgam of high and low art' (McNaughton, quoted in Falsetto, 2000, p. 330). The divergent reactions to *Henry* have therefore contributed to and been promoted by the very challenges that it poses to audiences, critics and regulators in working out how to categorize, think about and respond to it. It has no clear generic identity and is very careful in its selection of structural and stylistic devices in order to present its subject matter, position the viewer and locate itself within inter- and extratextual contexts precisely in order to avoid easy classification (Hantke, 2001; Rubin, 1992; Sconce, 1993; Pence, 1994).

As Marriott (2004) observes, the serial killer as 'chief bogeyman' of the second half of the twentieth century has been a popular subject for films, and he and Newman state that 'the serial killer is the movies' favourite monster' (2006, p. 213). Cettl (2003) takes this further, arguing that serial-killer films constitute a subgenre that carries its own set of operative narrative structures, character types, thematic bases and stylistic spectrum. He cites the Jack the Ripper murders as marking the beginning of the modern age of the serial killer, with the antecedents of the subgenre being rooted in horror (*M* (1931), *Psycho* (1960) *Peeping Tom* (1960)) and in crime films such as *Kiss of Death* (1947) and *The Naked City* (1948). Marriott (2004) points out the significance of *M* in eliminating the fantasy element from a horror film and *Psycho* and *Peeping Tom* as case studies that did not concern themselves with police procedure and gave their killers a relatively sympathetic face. Cettl (2003) outlines how *The Boston Strangler* (1968), which took its inspiration from the real-life serial killer Albert DeSalvo, signalled the splitting of the serial-killer film from its generic heritage and its emergence as a fully coded subgenre. This subgenre, Cettl argued, placed its emphasis on the police procedural of a manhunt within a case study, which introduced the role of the profiler.

What then followed, according to Cettl, was the splintering of this model in response to an increased focus in American culture on real and fictional random stranger violence. He identifies several splinters in a raft of films featuring repeat murderers: the spree killer (*Badlands* (1973); *Natural Born Killers*); the stalking psycho (*Blow Out* (1981); *Blue Steel* (1990)); the lone slasher (*Halloween* (1978), *Friday the 13th*); and the serial-killer film (*Henry*). Rubin supports this position, suggesting that a sub-subgenre of modern multiple murder films, starting with *The Honeymoon Killers* (1970) and followed by a small group of movies, including *Henry,* were characterized by 'bargain-basement budgets and under the floorboards subversiveness' and possessed a 'disturbing force' that distinguished them from more mainstream films (1992, p. 54). Other serial-killer films circulating mainly on video during the early 1980s and which caused controversy and/or ran into censorship problems in the UK included *The Driller Killer* (1979), *Maniac* (1980), *Don't Answer the Phone* (1981) and *Don't Go in the House* (1982). A consequence of the fragmentation of the serial-killer film, coupled with the wider controversies linked to specific films within the subgenre, has been the challenge which this poses for film distributors, exhibitors, viewers, critics and regulators seeking to position, market, interpret, classify and respond to *Henry*. This is not to imply that a genre or subgenre is fixed, static or a straitjacket, but it is nevertheless one key constitutive framework amongst several, including star and auteur, which help to shape film industry, film audience and film critical discourse relating to a particular movie.

In line with Simpson (2000) and Cettl (2003), it can be argued that *Henry* is a cross-genre mix of true-crime case study, *film noir*, horror film and road movie. Whilst working from a relatively stable generic base, *Henry* draws upon and subverts a number of stylistic and thematic elements from each genre or subgenre, leading to a range of key absences and presences within the film. For example, the absence within *Henry* of any police or effective law-enforcement officers results in Henry's invisibility to the authorities and his evasion of capture; the absence of any outside agency or profiler means that there are no behavioural or criminological frameworks within which to understand Henry's motives and actions; and the absence of any real clues to his behaviour denies audiences the pleasure of reading signs and identifying patterns in order to help decode meaning and identify motive (Simpson, 2000; Dyer, 1997; Cettl, 2003). Other features of *Henry* include an emphasis upon the mundane and everyday; a strong and sustained misogynistic violence, which can be read as morally objectionable and unacceptable; and the fact that no final retribution or justice is meted out to the central character (Simpson, 2000; Dyer, 1997; Cettl, 2003). These presences and absences help both to inflate and deflate certain familiar genre motifs associated with serial-killer films by deliberately setting up generic tensions within the film and decentring generic certainties (King, 2005). *Henry* has thus been contentious precisely because of the dynamic relationship that it has to a number of genres with which it aligns itself but into which it does not neatly fit. As Rubin (1992, p. 56) argues, the force of films like *Henry* derives from their falling into the cracks:

> They incompletely fill gaps left by moribund or decadent genres, and they lodge in the margins and borderlines of other, more contemporary genres. They are by no means out-side of genre; instead they hover around a wide range of generic contexts without settling comfortably in any of them.

Henry is not only difficult to situate within a fragmented serial-killer subgenre, it also draws upon and has subverted a range of structural and stylistic elements from various other genres and subgenres. This has resulted in *Henry* being hard to pin down and read generically, which has a potentially powerful distancing effect on viewers because it thwarts generic expectations and generates strong reactions. But this blending of genres and playing with audience expectations is also a potent source of pleasure for other audiences, reinforcing certain cultural tastes, dispositions and preferences (Sconce, 1993; Hill, 1997; King, 2005).

Text

The second section of this part builds upon the examination of *Henry's* production history and the preceding contextual analysis of genre to focus on how issues linked to narrative and form help to account for the debate sparked by the film. Notions of authenticity, realism and verisimilitude will also be touched upon in order to develop this analysis further.

Henry occupies a space within American cinema outside of Hollywood but linked to it, working as it does within and against Hollywood's generic, narrative and formal codes, conventions and thematic preoccupations. It is this positioning and the multiple tensions which it creates, both formally and thematically, which have significantly helped to promote controversy around *Henry* over time and in numerous different countries (Hantke, 2001; Pence, 1994).

Starting with narrative as a major formal dimension of film, it is suggested that, whilst working within the broad conventions of classical Hollywood narrative, *Henry* sought to challenge some of its codes. It is the tension between working both within and against normative modes of storytelling which prompted such a wide range of responses to *Henry* from audiences, thus highlighting the overlap between narrative mode and mode of reception. As King suggests, 'playing around with narrative can be a source of both pleasure and frustration, sometimes combined, depending on the orientation of both the individual films and viewers' (2005, p. 84). The extreme divergence in reactions to *Henry*, prompted by its approach to narrative, is one of the key factors contributing to the ongoing controversy attaching to the film. Whilst some audiences celebrated *Henry*'s narrative style, others were alienated by it. It is worth noting in passing that some forms of narrative are cheaper and easier to produce than others, and this may indicate another complicating dimension in the case of *Henry*, which some might be inclined to disparage as exploitation fare on precisely those grounds.

As a commercial and relatively mainstream film, *Henry* is part of a medium within which storytelling is a key guiding principle. Within American cinema, classical Hollywood narrative, recognized here as a range of tendencies rather than a set of absolutes, is the dominant storytelling paradigm (King, 2005). *Henry* offers its narrative within a form which is broadly recognizable to audiences versed in classical Hollywood narrative. For example, it has a conventional film narrative length (around eighty-six minutes) and a linear structure (both narratively and temporally); the narrative is organized around a central character and his relationship with two other characters; it is the film's characters who move the narrative forward; its opening scenes clearly reveal its main narrative and thematic concerns; and certain scenes, such as the murders of the fence and Otis, engage the stylized conventions of Hollywood violence. As a result of the film working broadly within the conventions of classical Hollywood narrative, audiences are in a position to comprehend the narrative of *Henry* by building the story (the actual events) from the plot (the way in which they are actually presented) even if they are not provided with the levels of story information or character motivation that they may expect.

On the other hand, *Henry* also challenges those same conventions. It does this by thwarting, displacing and short-circuiting its narrative dynamics in an attempt to revitalize the horror genre and subvert conventional modes of representing film violence. The result is that *Henry* undermines the narrative expectations of audiences, and this has been a crucial element in its controversy. According to King, an important feature of American independent cinema is that key aspects of classical Hollywood narrative are often undermined, minimized or complicated; as he puts it: 'In general, independent features are more likely to employ devices designed to deny, block, delay or complicate the anticipated development of narrative, to reduce clarity or resolution and in some cases to increase narrative self-consciousness' (2005, p. 63). Leaving this latter element aside for a moment, *Henry*'s contraventions of classical Hollywood narrative should be seen within the context of the rise of American independent film-making during the mid-1980s, and its tendency to borrow narrative and formal elements from European art, experimental and avant-garde cinemas. *Henry*'s deviations from classical form include a lack of an overarching narrative situation or enigma, an absence of a strong forward-moving drive or narrative quest, a low-key narrative structure that loosens the relationship between cause and effect and a concentration on the arbitrary, mundane and everyday over the spectacular: things seem just to happen and, when dramatic crises do occur, they are abrupt and tend to lack closure. Further narrative deviations include *Henry*'s emphasis on complex and ambiguous characters and their interrelationships; an almost documentary foregrounding of the characters' everyday milieu; the understatement of some of the murders (the hitch-hiker, Becky); and an oblique approach that plays down moral issues, final resolution, judgment and closure. Many of these narrative features, singularly, collectively and in combination, have provoked strong responses to *Henry* which, in turn, have helped to sustain and propagate debate around the film. So *Henry* offers a mode of storytelling, which, whilst drawing upon the narrative conventions of independent American and European art cinemas, contains them broadly within an overarching model of storytelling rooted within classical Hollywood narrative. In the final analysis, then, *Henry* offers an alternative mode of storytelling rather than subverting classical Hollywood narrative, as is sometimes claimed.

Turning briefly to narrative self-consciousness, it has been argued that the motivation for *Henry*'s narrative logic and formal treatment of character and situation lies in a desire for verisimilitude. According to King, a feature of *Henry*'s narrative is that

> Much of the focus is reoriented, away from the usual concerns of the serial killer narrative format, towards an emphasis on the more banal and everyday, and the everyday potential for violence in more 'normal' figures such as Otis (a reflection of the fact murder is usually a function of lives much more ordinary than the lurid fantasies of Hollywood serial killer movies). (2005, pp. 73–4)

This has proved to be a very contentious issue and has been a key driver in the controversy surrounding *Henry*. Others, including Taubin (1991) and Freeland (1995), have argued that there is a tension within *Henry* between its understated elements and the overstatement or stylization of other elements, including the murders of the family during the home invasion and the narrative focus upon Henry as the main character. This tension between, on the one hand, understatement and realism, and, on the other, stylization and spectacle, is another important factor in the ongoing discourse engendered by the film. This can be evidenced by the fact that some commentators are supportive of the perceived non-communicative and alienating elements of the film; others are highly critically of the seemingly misogynistic and class-based positions being advocated; whilst others still are split somewhere between the two positions. It has also been suggested that this perceived tension between verisimilitude and stylization can be read as a deliberate, unifying narrative device intended to draw attention to the highly constructed nature of narrative fiction and therefore the constructed assumptions and ideologies that support them (King, 2005). However, like so many claims about *Henry*, this is highly contentious.

In terms of the micro-formal aspects of *Henry*, whilst the film sought to use a range of formal approaches to create an impression of authenticity and departed from conventional storytelling techniques, it did so within conventional approaches to shooting and editing.[26] In this respect it conforms to King's dictum about independent film that 'formal innovation or departures tend to occur against a backdrop of relatively more familiar-conventional material, in the interests of comprehensibility and economic viability, in anything other than the work at the avant-garde end of the spectrum' (ibid., p. 161).

Henry's form is the result of a mixture of thematic motivations, economic imperatives and industrial inexperience. As such, it is *Henry*'s use of various formal devices to create the impression of authenticity, on the one hand, and, on the other, to foreground its departures from conventional and thus generally largely invisible formal techniques, which has led to much debate and difference of opinion. To complicate things still further, it is the combination of the tastes, preferences and dispositions that audiences bring to the text, along with the fact that it refuses to provide easy, reliable or reassuring answers, which has generated the wide divergence of opinion concerning *Henry* (Sconce, 1993).

Linked to *Henry*'s downplayed and understated narrative structure, the film engages a number of formal strategies in order to create the impression of authenticity. According to King (2005), independent American films tend to draw upon four approaches in order to create an impression of verisimilitude: a rejection of expensive production processes; the use of formal devices associated with documentary film-making; the claiming of actuality status; and the practice of particular acting styles. *Henry* employed elements of all four approaches in its pursuit of the impression of authenticity.

First, linked to issues of budget and industrial inexperience, the film-makers adopted an approach to the production of *Henry* that aligned itself with realist modes of film-making (small mobile crew, use of video and 16mm film, minimal lighting and a harsh sound mix). Second, *Henry* employed a range of representational codes and conventions associated more with drama-documentary than with *cinéma vérité*. According to Hallam and Marshment (2000), there is sufficient emphasis upon shot/reverse shot and point-of-view editing techniques to keep *Henry* within the conventions of fictional realism in spite of its static camerawork, sparse dialogue and the raw quality of the image. Moreover, for King (2005), *Henry*'s claims for unvarnished, de-dramatized realism come from realism of milieu rather than from the handheld camerawork. Meanwhile, Hallam and Marshment suggest that *Henry* is illustrative of what they refer to as 'expositional realism', which they suggest occurs 'where an episodic or picaresque narrative structure aims to explicate the relationship between characters and their environment' (2000, p. 101). They go on to suggest that *Henry* adopts a particular mode of expositional realism – one that offers a privileged view of the private world of a serial killer, a perspective that would not normally be focused upon in classical storytelling.

Third, *Henry* makes several claims to the status of actuality in an attempt to increase its perceived authenticity. The very title of the film, *Henry: Portrait of a Serial Killer*, offers a generic link to actuality, promising as it does insights into the life of a serial killer. This is further reinforced through the film's publicity and packaging, for example the tagline 'HE'S NOT FREDDY, HE'S NOT JASON ... HE'S REAL' and the employment on the video and DVD packaging of the photo of Henry self-reflexively staring at his reflection in a motel mirror. The film is also a retelling, albeit a fictionalized one, of the story of the real-life Henry Lee Lucas, and several of the film's tableaux were based upon crime-scene stills, including the 'Orange Socks' tableau that opens the film. However, as Rubin (1992) argues, although the film is based on real events, it is the *impression* of factuality in *Henry* which is more important than adherence to the actual facts. In other words, *Henry*'s relationship to real life is less about authenticity and factuality and more about qualities within the text itself. In this respect it is important, for example, that the settings of the film are actual locations rather than studio sets. Crucially, *Henry* draws upon what King (2005) refers to as a 'hierarchy of implied authenticity'. In other words, *Henry* constructs an impression of verisimilitude through the technological, formal and aesthetic features of 16mm film, which carries connotations of being more 'authentic' in representing the 'real' than 35mm film – which is often associated with professional and 'Hollywood' film-making. *Henry* also resorts to video footage at several key points in the film to deliver an even greater sense of actuality than the authenticity associated with grainy 16mm film stock.

Fourth, the film's production placed considerable emphasis upon the performative realism of its principal actors. This manifested itself in the casting of unknown theatre actors in the lead roles; in providing lengthy rehearsal time to help establish characters and build relationships; and in inviting the protagonists to contribute to the development of their characters based upon their own research into the case history of Lucas.

Viewer responses to this contrived impression of what has been variously referred to as realism, authenticity and verisimilitude suggest it is a major contributing factor to the controversy surrounding *Henry,* as the following quotes illustrate:

> Henry is exceptionally interesting – and also disturbing – for its realism of style and amoral viewpoint. ... It offers no audience identification figure, nor does its plot depict any righting of wrongs. ... [It] succeeds in creating terror and unease, both promising and withholding the spectacle of violence. (Freeland, 1995, p. 128)

> The film's principal virtue is its scrupulously realistic depiction of a serial killer. A disclaimer at the start avers that 'Henry is not intended to be an

accurate portrayal of a true story', similarities between the narrative and the real-life story of serial-killer Henry Lee Lucas notwithstanding, but it is authentic in a way that a number of 'real life' serial killer films – *Ed Gein* (2000), *Ted Bundy* (2002), *Gacy* (2003) – are not. (Marriott and Newman, 2006, p. 198)

Films which make the kinds of claims for authenticity which *Henry* does tend to be treated more seriously by viewers, as they are frequently seen as trying to say something about the 'real' world outside the fictional world of the film. This has provoked a variety of responses to *Henry* in relation to what viewers feel the film has to say about violence within society, and debate has focused upon what the film is perceived to be saying about the operations of power, violence, class, gender, sexuality and ethnicity. This has proved to be another significant factor in the controversy around the film. It also needs to be recognized that this discussion has taken place within the broader ongoing debate about the relationship of film to the real, as well as the wider concentric circle of argument about the nature of the real itself within contemporary global society.

Whilst *Henry* drew upon a number of approaches to create an impression of authenticity and was filmed and edited in a largely conventional way, the film also deviates formally from conventional storytelling in several key scenes. In these instances, rather than style being subordinate to narrative, in line with conventional film-making, formal devices deliberately call attention to themselves, particularly when compared with *Henry*'s otherwise downplayed narrative. As King suggests, 'Departures from dominant conventions are, generally, more visible than the conventions themselves, which often gain invisibility – through – familiarity' (2005, p. 84). Foregrounding form has the potential to open up awareness of formal mechanisms that usually remain beneath the level of attention. However, like the film's departures from conventional film-making in terms of narrative structure, these formal departures are contained within *Henry* by motivating factors that act as organizing principles.

Whilst an analysis of specific scenes that foreground form will be undertaken in the next chapter, a short examination of the film's five tableaux will be essayed here. The opening of *Henry* presents five tableaux of six murders. Formally, these tableaux undermine continuity editing and the conventions of classical narrative progression (King, 2005). This is achieved visually by extended shots, which move across the static aftermath of various murder scenes and which are accompanied by aural flashbacks documenting the murder. These tableaux do not function in a conventional way by revealing story information or driving the narrative forward towards an eventual resolution, but, rather, can be seen as adding to the general texture of uneasiness engendered by the film. At the same time, this formal strategy has the potential to have a powerful distancing effect on audiences, drawing attention to a departure from the normally invisible conventions of mainstream film-making.

These departures from conventional storytelling have fuelled the *Henry* debate and tend to be viewed in two distinct but related ways. First, as outlined above, by drawing direct attention to themselves, formal departures can be seen as having the critical potential to undermine dominant film-making conventions through generating a jarring, unsettling or distancing experience for viewers. This line of analysis is then often taken further to suggest that these distancing strategies have the potential to draw attention to ideological assumptions about violence in general in society, and serial killing and film violence in particular. For example, Freeland argues that 'the film is not fun to watch, but important because it forces viewers into reflection, questioning our cultural fascination with serial killers' (2008, p. 794), whilst Hantke takes this further by suggesting that

> An audience willing to abandon one model [mimetic] for the other [open and flexible] will find itself confronted with another layer of meaning, this one addressing not the rationale for the author's use of violence, or the lack thereof, but its own problematic enjoyment of these depictions of violence. (2001, p. 31)

A second approach, however, suggests that these formal flourishes in *Henry* are simply showy and exploitative, and merely exaggerate dominant film-making conventions. It has also been suggested that these departures are designed to provide a particular set of pleasures for viewers through the foregrounding of violent spectacle over narrative development. Certain critics, such as Taubin (1991), have also gone on to question the ideological position of *Henry*, suggesting that its departures from conventional film-making actually reveal a degree of misogyny. To complicate things further some critics (including Taubin) argue that certain of the film's formal departures, such as the tableaux, have the potential to raise questions about the relationship between film violence and violence in society whilst others are more exploitative and ideologically questionable, such as the home-invasion scene. Critical responses to *Henry*, which played a significant role in the controversy associated with the film also help to illustrate the overlap between the film's mode of reception and its formal properties (Sconce, 1993; Hallam and Marshment, 2000; King, 2005). We shall return to issues of form in the next part of the book.

Audience

This section examines the role of consumption and audience responses in drawing upon, engaging with and also perpetuating the debate sparked by *Henry*. Hill (1997) carried out a small-scale, in-depth, qualitative study in the UK to help understand why audiences choose to watch violent films and in so doing explored the process of viewing fictional violence. Hill's study is particularly significant to an understanding in this case because, at a time when films characterized as examples of the 'new brutalism' were controversial,[27] *Henry* featured specifically. Hill's work was an attempt to find a way of productively discussing, outside the usual cause-and-effect debates, film violence and its consumption.

Hill argues that audiences possess 'portfolios of interpretation'. These portfolios describe the ways in which audiences actively understand and

interpret violent films and, in so doing, build up a range of responses to film
violence as part of the viewing process. For Hill, audiences utilize a number of
reactive mechanisms to help them to interpret and understand film violence,
including anticipation, building character relationships, self-censoring and
testing boundaries. She explains that the key to the process of viewing
violence is the context of viewing and the recognition that viewing violence is
a social activity in which viewers consciously test boundaries, safe in the
knowledge that the text is fictional and separate from actual violence within
society. By developing such portfolios of interpretation, audiences of violent
movies demonstrate how complex and dynamic the process of viewing can
actually be, and, based upon these portfolios, Hill developed a model of the
viewing process. This isolates four linked groups of factors that shape
responses to fictional film violence: 'pre-viewing contextual factors',
'pre-viewing individual factors', 'within viewing contextual factors' and 'within
viewing individual factors' (ibid, pp. 109–11). Hill suggests that this model
can help audiences, researchers, policy makers and regulators to understand
and predict viewers' responses to fictional film violence.

Hill's model offers valuable insights into how audiences' active
consumption of *Henry* has been framed by, but has also contributed to, the
generation, circulation and maintenance of controversy surrounding the film.
Whilst several pre-viewing contextual factors have been examined in other parts
of this book, two factors outlined by Hill will be analysed here in order to
underline their potential to offer constitutive frameworks for audience responses
to *Henry*: social/normative notions of the acceptability of violent images, and
cinemagoing/video viewing as learned social behaviour. Consumers of film
violence who are interested in *Henry* are, to varying degrees, very aware of the
overlaps between the commercial marketing of the film, the hype and
controversy that it generated and its official regulatory history. Audiences,
particularly within the UK context, are also aware of the cultural forms of
regulation operating through moral panics and what Barker (1995) calls
'discourses of danger' about levels of unacceptable fictional violence. As a result,
audiences' pre-viewing thoughts about *Henry* would in all likelihood be moulded

by a range of contextual factors, and these impressions would then go on to play a part in the perpetuation and maintenance of the debate about the film.

Pre-viewing individual factors intersect with pre-viewing contextual factors to help establish audience members' expectations of *Henry* and also anticipate their possible reactions to the film. Hill outlines four pre-viewing individual factors: understanding of fictional violence as entertainment, perceptions of real violence, anticipation and developed thresholds. Her study shows how viewers made distinctions between real violence, mediated real violence and fictional violence, with participants reporting how they felt appalled by the rawness of real violence and found that mediated real violence, which was influenced stylistically by fictional violence, was not entertaining. A similar finding was also reported by Kimber (2000). However, Hill's participants stated that fictional violence was entertaining partly because of the effects of the distancing mechanisms of mediation and stylization in its representations of violence, a point supported by Prince (2000) and Potter (1999). This had important implications for *Henry*, which was not seen as entertaining, despite containing fictional violence, because of what participants saw as its 'documentary realism'. As participant 1 – FG6 stated:

> When I watched *Henry: Portrait of a Serial Killer* it wasn't so much the scenes themselves that I considered extremely violent, as the way in which they came across. I felt I had actually witnessed violence. Most other films the violence is glossed over, or done with a sense of humour to take the edge off it so that it doesn't leave you too shell-shocked. The thing is, if you actually see violence for what it is, it is horrific'. (quoted in Hill, 1997, p. 83)

This line of approach is taken further by rbsv (2004) on the Internet Movie Database:[28]

> I can count on one hand the films that I have found to be so deeply disturbing, that I later regretted seeing them. This film is among them …

> I honestly felt as though I had actually witnessed several murders. I was really shaken by the horrific realism of this cinematic event. This film was so powerfully upsetting for me, that I feel a need to warn others of the emotional impact.

The perceived realism of the film aligned it more with real and mediated real violence and made *Henry* more disturbing for that reason. Hill states that *Henry* was one of the least popular choices in the target films explored in her project, a trend mirrored by UK box-office figures and video rentals. *Henry* challenged participants' thresholds, either social or personal, in the matter of fictional representations of film violence, as illustrated by Cornetarquin (2005):

> I have never felt so sick watching a film before. Its violence was so gratuitous that I found it hard to believe what I was watching. There is enough real life sickness without film makers wallowing in an orgy of violence like they did in this waste of celluloid. I think anyone connected with this tripe should feel ashamed of themselves.

Similarly lizcarran (2007) states that:

> I watched this and turned off half way through. I was so sickened by what I saw. Regretfully curiosity got the better of me and I watched the rest of it which was just as sick, perverse, cruel and ghastly as the first part. ... It's a revolting film, I really hate it. ... There is nothing good to say about it.

However, some audience members, who were aware of the controversy associated with *Henry* and had an interest in contentious films, actively sought it out in order to test their own boundaries and thresholds, precisely because of the perceived realism of the film's violence. For some Henry did not live up to the hype, as Andrews's response (2007) demonstrates:

> This is apparently a controversial film … but I'm not so sure why
> because I thought it was all right but nothing more. … It just portrays
> Henry and the people around him going about their normal boring
> everyday life. Now this sort of thing obviously excites some as *Henry:
> Portrait of a Serial Killer* is a well regarded film although I was thoroughly
> bored.

The accumulation of pre-viewing contextual and individual factors
predisposes audiences to have certain expectations of *Henry* and fosters widely
differing responses, from a need to see the film uncut, to not wanting to see
specific parts of the film, to avoiding it completely or to being disappointed by
it. This clearly demonstrates how responses to *Henry* are shaped by awareness
of its controversial nature, which in turn helps either to rework, play down or
perpetuate them.

With respect to the within viewing contextual factors, Hill's model
outlines three of these: the safety of the cinema, the context of the event
as a social activity and the film as a testing experience. Hill's findings
suggest that certain audiences prefer to view challenging films at the
cinema as a way of keeping potentially disturbing material out of the
private domain of the home. However, she also found that the increased
possibilities for self-censorship afforded by the home (leaving the room,
turning the film off and/or fast-forwarding challenging scenes or
sequences) made it a preferred viewing venue for others. She discovered
that more participants watched *Henry* at home than in the cinema,
although this may have been a consequence of the film's limited theatrical
release in the UK. According to Hill, audiences are aware of those around
them when viewing violent films and they gauge their responses in the light
of the responses of others. This raised discussions around appropriate and
inappropriate responses to *Henry*. Participants felt that, whilst it was
acceptable to laugh at the violence in *Pulp Fiction*, it was not appropriate to
laugh at the violence in *Henry*. A similar response was reported by
ba.harrison (2007) on IMDB:

Nearly twenty years ago, I caught this film at an all-night horror film festival. Instead of the whooping, hollering and cheering that accompanied most of the other movies, *Henry* was met with deadly silence by the audience … everyone watching was lost for words.

There are overlaps here with pre-viewing contextual factors and pre-viewing individual factors aligned to personal views on violence as entertainment, and in particular what are regarded as socially acceptable levels of fictional violence. *Henry* was seen as a particularly testing film because of the way in which it provokes very personal responses to social thresholds and taboos linked to film violence. For example, Hill's participants cited the representation of sexual violence and rape in *Henry* as being particularly shocking, with some respondents feeling that it was quite unacceptable whilst others argued that boundaries are there to be pushed. More generally, participants reported that they found violence against children and the use of everyday weapons such as knives, to carry out interpersonal acts of violence particularly disturbing. It is interesting to note that in the UK the third tableau was initially cut not only for sexual violence but also because a bottle had served as a weapon; the 'shopping' scene was cut to remove details of violence employing household items; and the home-invasion scene was cut to remove not only sexual violence but the use of a knife. This illustrates a clear articulation between cultural, official and self-imposed forms of regulation. Official forms of regulation are not only informed by cultural fears regarding the consumption of film violence, they also institutionalize them in classification guidelines and laws. These institutionalized fears then become frameworks that individuals inculcate and draw upon when making decisions about violent films, thus further embedding cultural fears about film violence in an ongoing cycle (Kimber, 2000).

According to Hill's model, within viewing individual factors include anticipation, building character relationships, thresholds, self-censorship and boundary testing. For Hill, anticipation is central to the emotional and physical responses of audiences to film violence, constituting part of the enjoyment of its consumption. Viewers play a game, anticipating the worst by reading aural and visual clues in the text and, if not watching alone, being aware of and responding to the reactions of those around them.

Henry has the potential to 'win' this game by making it difficult to anticipate what will happen next and by offering representations of violence, which, whilst not real, resonate with audiences' perceptions of real violence, which of course are themselves framed by mediated representations of that violence (Potter, 1999). This can shock and alienate some viewers, thus fuelling further controversy. For others, *Henry* is pleasurable precisely because it is difficult to read and predict, hence raising expectations and heightening anticipation of the visceral shocks that it presents. As dee.reid (2008) comments:

> What is great about *Henry: Portrait of a Serial Killer* is the brutal and uncompromising presentation of the story – the stark, frightening realism of the events, the raw intensity, brutality and utter savagery of everything we are forced to see here.

However, these particular pleasures can also stir up debate because of the way they epitomize what may be seen by some as 'problematic' responses to violent films. During Hill's study, she showed participants a scene in which Becky stabs Otis in the eye with the handle of a comb and Henry murders him. For Hill, this revealed interesting data on within viewing individual factors. Hill's participants were asked if they identified with any of the characters in the scene. They reported that they did not identify with specific characters but that they did develop relationships with characters. The types of relationships that participants formed with characters were based on several factors, including context within the narrative, characterization, personal preferences (was the character's violence justified or unjustified?), experiences of real violence and imaginative hypothesizing (what would I do in that position?). Audience feedback revealed that Henry was the most popular character in the scene and that his actions were felt to be understandable within the context of the scene. Moreover, participants developed their relationship with Henry by anticipating and preparing for his violent actions. Hill suggests that whilst nobody actually wants to be Henry, this does not stop spectators building a relationship with him within the safe environment of a fictional film. Otis was read in relation to Henry and was generally hated by participants. There was, however, some sympathy for him on account of the violence of his death, signified by his screaming, but this did not lead to identification with him; audiences distanced themselves from Otis out of self-preservation, an attempt to protect themselves from being shocked, disturbed or upset by his actions.

The majority of participants, male and female, had sympathy for Becky but chose not to develop a relationship with her, although reasons for not doing so divided along gender lines: women shut themselves off from Becky out of self-preservation whilst men felt that she would not have acted so violently in that situation. What this reveals is that audiences have complex and personal responses to scenes of violence and violent films. As such, their responses should not be reduced to a homogenous understanding that they unproblematically 'identify' with violent characters in films.

According to Hill, individual thresholds (the level at which a person finds representations of fictional violence disturbing, which is based upon personal experience and which is specific to that viewer) can and will have a major impact on how a viewer responds emotionally and physically to film violence. Whilst it is difficult to generalize about this, *Henry* has the potential to test audiences' thresholds on a number of levels, and this can lead to a range of reactive measures including self-censorship. The key element here is distance: Hill found that if fictional violence was stylized it was often seen as more acceptable and as offering a safe environment in which audiences could build relationships with characters and have more emotional involvement in the film, secure in the knowledge that this would have little effect on real life. However, where this distance was not perceived to exist, as in *Henry*, participants often reported that they did not want to become involved directly or deeply because the film was too close to real-life events and, as such, was too painful, disturbing and potentially shocking to them. These personal responses, framed by wider contexts, have the potential to rework and perpetuate the controversy, and the discourses of revulsion and admiration, surrounding *Henry*.

Within Hill's model, self-censorship is based upon consumer choice, audience expectation and boundary testing. She outlines the four modes of self-censorship, namely the self-censorship of all violent movies, of violent movies containing thresholds, of violent scenes containing thresholds and of violent images containing thresholds (Hill, 1997, p. 60). Audiences actively select a range of modes of self-censorship appropriate to their perceived level of anticipation of the film violence to be experienced. For Hill, this anticipation and preparation lead to an exploration of the feelings provoked by film violence within the safe environment of a fictional world and are a key part of the process of viewing violence. Methods of self-censorship include creating physical barriers (hiding face, covering ears) and mental ones (thinking about something else or reminding oneself that it is just a film). Some of the scenes, sequences and images in *Henry* can indeed produce intense emotional and physical responses. As Hill points out:

> When participants saw a scene from *Henry* ... they exhibited distinctive bodily reactions: participants touched their eyes, ears, covered their mouths, steeled themselves and showed tense facial muscles. Not only did participants exhibit such responses during the screenings, the memory of certain violent images was so strong many participants re-enacted their physical response during the discussion. (ibid., p. 32)

This reveals the importance of boundary testing as a constituent part of the consumption of film violence – the interpretation of responses to fictional film violence by testing reactions to it. Thresholds and self-censorship demonstrate boundary testing, and it is via such testing that thresholds are identified and self-censorship employed. Hill's findings suggest that, while audiences want to be tested, many spectators do not want to be tested too much. This is not to minimize, however, the pleasures which some audiences gain from watching films that present challenging and confrontational representations of fictional film violence. According to John Lindsey (2006):

> The movie is one of the greatest and most important movies of the horror genre, it is no mere slasher flick but a dark and brooding psychopath movie with fantastic acting and thoughts as well as some truly disturbing murder sequences that make you want to keep the lights on at night.

What this quote reveals is a certain kind of response from audience members who experienced a degree of pleasure through the film's testing of their own personal thresholds. However, for them, the film comes *close* to pushing them across a wider social threshold ('keep[ing] the lights on at night') without *actually* transgressing it (since *Henry* makes them 'want to' keep the lights on, without necessitating the further step of enacting such a mechanism of self-censorship). The participants within Hill's study were, on the one hand, fascinated by *Henry* and found it an interesting and challenging film but, on the other, suggested that it was too real and too challenging to be entertaining or a candidate for repeat viewing. What this exercise in audience research demonstrates is that spectators' active responses to Henry, whilst informed by prior knowledge of the controversy attaching to it, are also shaped by numerous other, personal factors.

This chapter has taken a range of key debates about both independent cinema and violence in films and evaluated their contributions to the way *Henry* has been perceived. It would seem that *Henry* has been controversial precisely because it engaged so directly and provocatively with a number of social, cultural and political fissures; worked within and against Hollywood's generic, narrative and formal codes, conventions and thematic preoccupations; and possesses the potential to test audiences' thresholds and boundaries. The next chapter will take some of these points forward into a textual analysis of three scenes that are central to the debate aroused by the film.

✖ PART 4

KEY SCENE ANALYSIS

This section takes three key scenes from the 1998 MPI US Director's Edition DVD of *Henry*[29] and subjects them to close textual analysis, with the aim of examining their part in fuelling the debate linked to the film. The first scene, from the second chapter, 'The Exterminator', is the third tableau, which concerns a murdered prostitute. The second, from the eighth chapter, 'Let's Go Shopping', involves Henry and Otis murdering the fence. The third, from the tenth chapter, 'Home Invasion', shows Henry and Otis breaking into a suburban house and murdering a middle-class family. These scenes have been selected for several reasons: their centrality to censorial and classificatory controversy in the UK and US; their significance within academic, critical and fan discourses; their provocative play with formal, generic and narrative codes and conventions; their potential to test audience boundaries; and their centrality to McNaughton and Fire's stated vision. Whilst the identification and isolation of specific scenes or moments for this kind of analysis does admittedly involve a certain level of de- and re-contextualization of meaning, it can nonetheless play an important evaluative role.

Textual analysis seeks to develop an understanding of the meanings generated by texts through the scrutiny of signifying practices assessed within a range of overlapping textual, intertextual and extratextual contexts. The aim of this critical practice is to develop an understanding of how a film, in this case *Henry*, has been constructed through the collaborative processes of textual production (encoding), and of how it may be interpreted and engaged by a range of audiences to make sense of the world which both they and the text inhabit (decoding). Textual analysis is an approach used across numerous academic disciplines including sociology, cultural studies, media studies and film studies. Researchers working within these different disciplines often adopt, hardly surprisingly, different theoretical and methodological approaches to the analysis of texts. The textual analysis undertaken here of the key scenes in *Henry* draws upon a hybridization of micro and macro approaches. The micro analysis focuses on how meanings are formally and thematically constructed within the scenes, examining the interrelationships between, for example, *mise-en-scène*, editing, soundtrack, dialogue and acting. The macro analysis seeks to develop an understanding of how the meanings constructed within each scene work across the film and within the wider intertextual and extratextual contexts of production and reception. This is not to suggest that there is one definitive reading of these scenes or that there is only one way of approaching the textual analysis of films; instead, what is offered is an approach to the analysis of contentious scenes which could also be employed in the study of other controversial films.

The analysis of the key scenes develops an argument structured around four interconnected strands, building upon several areas examined in the preceding chapter, namely genre, violence, narrative, visual and reception. First, *Henry* uses violence to structure the design of the film stylistically and narratively and to arrange spectators' emotional responses to that violence in what Kinder calls a 'narrative orchestration of violent attractions' (2001, p. 63). Second, *Henry*'s mode of orchestrating these attractions is one which 'moves the viewer through a gradually intensified spectacle into climax and denouement' (Freeland, 1995, p. 132). Third, *Henry* juxtaposes different categories of film violence, categories which have been variously described via the oppositions of weak/strong (McKinney, 1993) turn on /turn off (Corner, 1998) and depicted/authentic (Morrison *et al.*, 1999). Fourth, *Henry* has been constructed formally and thematically to include distanciation devices that operate to disorientate and alienate viewers through the de-normalization of cinematic practices and of the wider social relations that these practices help to normalize – for example, power or gender relations. By drawing attention to themselves and distancing audiences, these devices have the potential to encourage spectators to reflect upon their consumption of film violence and its associated pleasures and displeasures. Examination of these strands, taken together, leads to the conclusion that *Henry* exploits rather than simply employs film violence (Hantke, 2001) and that this is why it has evoked the kind of polarized reactions that have helped to generate and perpetuate the controversy surrounding the film.

The Third Tableau

As already noted, *Henry* contains five tableaux. Four occur within the first six minutes of the film and the fifth takes place a little after fifteen minutes. Pinedo (1997) suggests that the montage of scenes which makes up the start of the film establishes both Henry as the organizing centre of the narrative and his life as both violent and mundane. For Pinedo, 'the unpredictability of the film set up by the opening sequence means that ... the outcome is always in question' (1997, p. 100). The third tableau takes place four minutes sixteen seconds into the film and lasts thirty-nine seconds. It has been selected for analysis because of the controversy that it sparked, particularly in the UK where, as we have seen, distributors themselves censored it from the film between 1991 and 2003.[30]

The scene is set in an unidentified motel room and reveals the aftermath of the murder of an anonymous prostitute whilst simultaneously playing the audience an aural flashback documenting the attack. In terms of *Henry*'s narrative orchestration of violent attractions, the tableau plays a role in establishing the film's gory nature but withholds the spectacle of the actual murder. No contextualization is offered for the murder: the tableau is sandwiched between two scenes of Henry merely driving alone, first along an urban street, then on the interstate. The song 'La Lania' acts as a sound bridge between the two driving scenes, although the transition is not seamless, implying a temporal break. The placing of the tableau between these scenes illustrates Rubin's (1992) point that, in films such as *Henry*, conventional 'suspenseful' build-ups to violence are generally avoided in favour of an arbitrary suddenness or flat inevitability.

The asynchronous relationship between sound and image acts as a distancing device by fracturing the reality effect and splitting the seamlessness that conventionally exists between sound and image (Taubin, 1991). In this way, *Henry* arouses and then refuses to satisfy the desire to know exactly what has happened/is happening, leading to what Abbott calls 'narrative jamming', where 'certain narrative questions arise without leading to any clear understanding of what is going on' (2002, p. 10). The effect of this particular distanciation device is to make spectators aware that they are watching an illusion, thus momentarily fracturing identification. According to Rubin: 'The general anti-expressiveness [of films like *Henry*] is augmented with specific devices that trouble the creation of homogeneous realism' (1992, p. 56). This encourages audiences to reflect upon dominant representations of Hollywood film violence and the generic conventions associated with horror films, by drawing their attention to what it looks and sounds like when film violence is not represented in the conventional way.

The camera slowly tracks in one continuous shot from left to right across the motel room, from a starting position looking at an unmade bed covered in white, bloodstained sheets. The camera, from no particular point of view, pans to the right and tilts up as it passes a bedside table. The table holds a phone, lamp, ashtray (containing a partially smoked cigarette) and a book of matches. The camera continues to track through a door frame which connects bedroom and bathroom. The subdued lighting of the bedroom coupled with the rich colours (the leather bed surround, the heavy drapes tied back behind the bed, the dark colouring of the back wall, the wooden bedside table, the dark beams and door frame) contrast with the brightly neon-lit bathroom (with its white floor and wall tiles and turquoise bathroom suite with chrome and glass fittings). As the camera enters the bathroom, the body of a dead, semi-naked woman wearing lingerie (black knickers, red suspender belt, a black fishnet stocking, a single red stiletto and a half-removed black bra) is revealed slumped on a toilet. The camera slowly tilts up as it tracks in on the woman, moving from a long shot of her body from the neck down to a medium close-up of her head and face. The woman's head is not revealed until twenty-three seconds into the thirty-nine-second scene and at no point is her whole body shown. She has a cut on her right cheek and a broken, clear-glass

The shot of the dead prostitute which ends the third tableau.

bottle impaled in the left side of her mouth. Her left wrist is tied with white tape to the frame supporting the wash basin and her right wrist is bound to a towel rack with her other stocking. There is blood around the wound on her face, on her neck, on her left shoulder and between her partially exposed breasts, as well as on the basin and floor. The camera is still moving in on the woman's face as the scene cuts to Henry driving along the freeway.

Aurally, the scene presents a rich and progressively more distorted soundscape by layering and mixing a range of diegetic and non-diegetic sound effects, music and snippets of distorted dialogue. The tableau starts with the diegetic sound of running water, which persists throughout the whole scene and which is revealed to emanate from a running tap in the bathroom. Shortly after the start of the tableau, the non-diegetic 'Dead Body Drone', which had accompanied the previous tableaux, starts up and runs through the rest of the scene, acting as a sound bridge. As the camera passes the telephone, the sound of a ringing phone can be heard. A woman's non-diegetic and erotically charged voice is heard saying 'Oh baby!' and the phone rings again. There is also the non-diegetic sound of heavy breathing. Now in the bathroom, the line 'Oh baby!' is heard again, but this time distorted and louder. As the camera tracks in on and tilts up the dead woman's body, the sound mix becomes louder and more frenetic. There are non-diegetic muffled sounds in the background and a man's voice is heard shouting 'Shut up! Shut up!' There is the non-diegetic sound of breaking glass and a woman's distorted screams. The man's voice is heard again shouting 'Die, bitch!' whilst the phone rings and there are more distorted female screams, before a man's voice shouts 'Die! Die! Die!' More distorted screams follow, mixed with sounds of heavy breathing, before the film cuts to Henry driving along a freeway.

This dissonance between sound and image also serves to disrupt temporal relationships within the scene, thus dislocating continuity. This acts as a second distanciation device drawing attention to the constructed illusion of reality manufactured through continuity editing in classical narrative cinema. As a direct result of the images of the scene representing an assumed present (the gradual revealing of a murdered woman's body) and the soundtrack representing an aural flashback (which offers insight into what has happened some time in the past), the constructed nature of cinema is effectively laid bare. As Pinedo puts it: 'The temporal disjunction between the present of the visual track and the past of the sound track is unsettling and disorientating … the muted sound track simultaneously reveals and withholds the violent encounter' (1997, p. 100). Pinedo further suggests that *Henry* subverts horror cinema's traditional model of 'recreational terror', which works within the dialectic of seeing (the spectacle of the ruined body) and not seeing (delayed, partial, blocked vision and (or) absence of the killer), and replaces not seeing with not hearing (muted, distorted, muffled sounds). I want to complicate this by suggesting that the film does not in fact replace not seeing with not hearing, but, rather, it uses not seeing (the slow reveal of the woman's ruined body and face and the absence of the killer), not hearing (overlaid muted, distorted and blended dialogue, music and sound effects) and seeing (the slow track in on the woman's mutilated face) to enhance the affective and estranging qualities of the scene.

As suggested in the previous chapter, departures from conventional film-making practices such as those identifiable within the third tableau are often the exception rather than the norm in mainstream films, and they are generally formally and thematically motivated. To see the aftermath of the murder of the prostitute whilst listening to an aural flashback of her death can be read as being formally motivated, implying that the killings are hidden in between the very conventions of continuity editing. Thematically, this tableau is motivated by and also fits into *Henry*'s implication that serial murder is often concealed within the banal texture of everyday life and that, as a result, it often goes undetected by the authorities. The use of such a device further encourages spectators to reflect upon the constructed nature of film violence, as revealed through the disruption of continuity editing, and also upon their own motives for watching film violence.

A third distanciation device present in the third tableau is an operative modality, which, whilst stylized, signifies seriousness through the use of 'turn off', 'authentic' and 'strong' representations of film violence. In terms of modality (the relationship between a text and reality), the stylization (often recognized as ameliorating the affective impact of film violence, particularly within genre films) of this tableau here has the potential to assault the sensibilities by signifying directness and immediacy within the diegesis. 'Turn off' violence, for Corner (1998), is violence that is shown to take place within the moral framings of everyday life, so that a degree of unpleasantness, disturbance and even distress will accompany the viewing. Corner acknowledges that this type of violence can lead to problems with regulators and viewers, as indeed was the case with *Henry* in the UK.

According to audience research carried out by David Morrison *et al.* (1999), the process whereby audiences come to define a film as violent involves the workings of two 'definers'. A 'primary definer', which must be present for the 'secondary definer' to be utilized, is a moral consideration about whether the violence is appropriate, fair or justified. As Hill (1997) outlined in her model of the viewing process of violent films, such boundaries and thresholds can be social or individual. If film violence breaches moral thresholds and boundaries then the second, aesthetic, definer is brought into play, which has to do with whether the violence looks real in the sense of being true to life or real in the sense of being mediated through aesthetic codes of realism. The violence within this scene has the potential to be categorized as 'authentic' violence, in that it is random, set in an everyday context, and is capable of assaulting the sensibilities of those who watch it (Morrison *et al.*, 1999). The authenticity of the violence is the result of several related factors, including: the lack of any narrative explanation for the graphic, sexualized and misogynistic murder of a woman at the hands of a male serial killer; the affective qualities of the highly stylized representation of the aftermath of the murder, deploying dissonant visual and aural techniques; and the cumulative impact of the distancing devices employed in this and the other tableaux. For McKinney (1993), 'strong' violence describes film violence that has depth of meaning, serves a narrative purpose and encourages audiences to be active by generating in them a range of emotional and moral responses. He suggests that, 'like all works of strong violence, it [*Henry*] leaves an audience feeling dead inside, yet, somehow, more alive than it was two hours before' (1993, p. 19). 'Strong' violence is enlisted here, in association with the other distanciation devices, to encourage audiences to think about the (dis)pleasures associated with the (il)legitimacy and (non)justification of the fictional violence in the tableau.

Of course, not all audiences will respond in the same way to the third tableau, but this analysis may go some way to accounting for the regulatory and critical controversy prompted by this scene and for its place within *Henry*'s overall mode of narratively orchestrating its violent attractions.

Alternative views on the third tableau include those of Sconce (1993), who suggests that all the tableaux in *Henry* produce a certain form of identification in cine-literate audiences. He argues that the tableaux' pronounced use of certain self-reflexive cinematic techniques functions as a form of highly self-conscious 'artistic' narration that directly appealed to certain critics and cinephiles, inviting them to read the film 'artistically' and thus encouraging a specific form of identification between themselves, the text and particularly the director. For Sconce, *Henry*'s explicit promotion of pleasures that appealed directly to these elite, adult-taste cultures resulted in them championing the film as a consequence of the intensification of viewer identification rather than any subversion of these dominant patterns, whilst simultaneously reinforcing their own cultural dispositions and preferences over those of other film audiences.

It could also be suggested that the third tableau affords spectators the opportunity to indulge in what Dyer refers to as 'sadistic visual pleasure' (1997, p. 17). Dyer's reflections on the murder of a woman in *Maniac* raise several questions that can equally be asked of the third tableau:

> Are we to identify with her and her terror, either to remember just how terrible serial killing is, or else to experience fear vicariously, as masochistic thrill? Or are we simply to enjoy watching [hearing] her suffer? And who does the film think 'we' are, men or women? (ibid.)

In fact, this quotation raises a number of questions that could also be asked of several other scenes in *Henry*, including those involving the murder of two prostitutes in Henry's car, the murder and molestation of the mother during the home invasion, and the rape and eventual off-screen murder of Becky at the end of the film (Taubin, 1991).

'Let's Go Shopping'

The 'Let's Go Shopping' scene takes place forty minutes twenty-two seconds into the film and lasts three minutes ten seconds. It has been singled out for analysis on account of its significance within *Henry*'s narrative orchestration of violent attractions and also because it was cut in the UK to remove 'process'

violence when it was first released on video. In terms of its orchestration, as
Freeland (1995) suggests, the scene reflects the film's mode of slowly revealing
violent spectacle. The scene also plays with viewers' emotions by representing
a vicious and gruesome killing in a manner underscored by comedy.

Otis, having kicked in the flickering black-and-white TV in his
apartment, declares to Henry, after being challenged about his behaviour:
'Shit. I just got to have a TV', to which Henry replies: 'Well, let's go shopping.'
During the scene, Henry and Otis visit a fence in a backstreet warehouse to
buy a TV with $50. Otis and Henry are shown a range of audiovisual
equipment but, when they decide to buy the first $50 set that they had been
offered, an argument ensues, as the fence feels that his time has been wasted.
As the argument escalates, Henry and Otis stab the fence repeatedly with a
soldering iron, strangle him with a cable, smash the $50 TV set over his head,
turn it on and electrocute him. The scene then cuts to Henry, Otis and Becky

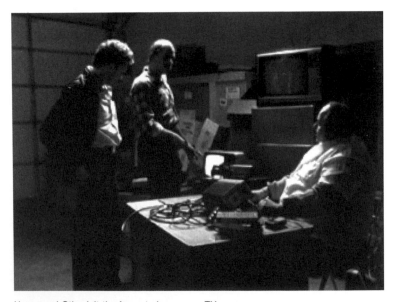

Henry and Otis visit the fence to buy a new TV.

making a home video in their apartment with equipment stolen from the fence. Unlike the third tableau, the 'shopping' scene is constructed around a conventional Hollywood suspense build-up, which invites us to sit back, enjoy and even to see the funny side of the action, which is fully contextualized and motivated within the film's narrative.

Formally and thematically, the scene constructs moments of fictional violence which can be read as legitimate, justified and therefore acceptable within the generic conventions of the serial-killer or horror film. In part this is because the character of the fence is constructed in several complementary ways as a relatively legitimate target for violence. First, there is his anonymity: within the scene the fence is not referred to by name (his appellation comes solely from the film's credits). As Hill (1997) pointed out, the way in which audiences build relationships with characters in violent films is fluid and negotiated, and because Henry and Otis are at the narrative centre of the film, our sympathies tend to lie more with them than with the fence, who is not as significant within the wider narrative and of whom we have no prior knowledge, thus making it possible for us to choose not to develop a relationship with him. Second, his generic characterization as a dealer in stolen goods, and the implied links to the criminal underworld, can lead us to distance ourselves from him within the narrative or to anticipate that something unpleasant will happen to him. Third, the way in which he is filmed (framed by high-angle shots looking down on him in his seated position) makes the viewer feel more powerful than the character and/or detached from him. By contrast, the low-angle shots that frame Henry and Otis exaggerate their importance and thus formally encode the power relations between the characters, as well as between them and us. Fourth, the physical appearance of the fence (overweight, unkempt and generally unattractive) acts as a generic cue to us that this particular character may not be around for too long. Fifth, the fence's behaviour constructs him as a relatively legitimate target for violence, becoming increasingly abusive as his frustration with Otis and Henry mounts:

FENCE: (*shouting*) What's the matter? You got shit in your ears? The black and white is 50 dollars, take it or leave it.

HENRY: Sorry we wasted your time, come on Otis.

FENCE: Don't give me sorry, you dumb ass! Did I stutter?! Give me the 50 dollars and get out! (*Hits table with hand*)

HENRY: I'll give you 50 bucks!

Sixth, in generic terms the violence takes place between fellow criminals and, within such a milieu, the fence could be seen as deserving his fate for biting off more than he can chew by taking on Henry and Otis. Moreover, because Henry and Otis initially exhibit some restraint, something not extended to their other victims, their actions could be seen as more acceptable than in other violent scenes in that they are responding to the escalating provocations of the fence rather than inflicting random violence on a complete stranger.

The violence in this scene is framed by an operative modality that de-emphasizes seriousness and threat and utilizes 'turn on' and 'weak' representations of violence. According to King (2004), the affective impact of film violence can be ameliorated through the use of three overlapping formal and thematic devices, which can construct a non-serious modality, and this scene demonstrates all three: violent spectacle and the stylized aestheticization of film violence; the generic conventions of the serial-killer or horror film, within which violence is part of the anticipated repertoire; and comedy, in particular the use of conventions associated with cartoons or slapstick. These factors in combination allow the violence within the scene to be more entertaining, even amusing, than threatening.

'Turn on' violence, for Corner (1998), is violence represented in a way that provides excitement via heightened action, intensified character performance and special effects. According to McKinney (1993), 'weak' violence is characterized as having surface meaning only, serving no narrative purpose and having no impact because it does not evoke any emotional engagement or moral response. For McKinney, 'weak' violence is conservative in the sense that its main function is to reinforce and not challenge the status quo, and it is present in most films. Applying to this scene the primary and secondary definers mentioned earlier, it can be argued that, whilst the violence pushes the boundaries of acceptability, it is also mitigated by its conventional Hollywood stylization, its adherence to generic conventions, and its comic elements.

However, the scene does explicitly represent several acts of physical injury. The first of these is shown in the extreme close-up of the stabbing of the fence's hand with a soldering iron. Henry then stabs the fence with the iron in the chest and stomach four times, twice clearly and twice in a more fumbled manner, blood seeping through his white shirt. Otis grapples with and then strangles the fence with the cord of the video recorder, after which Henry smashes the $50 TV onto the head of the bewildered and heavily breathing fence before instructing Otis to plug in the device, thus electrocuting him. As the TV is smashed onto the fence's head, blood pours down his face and onto his already bloodied shirt. During this scene the fence

After being strangled and repeatedly stabbed, the fence is electrocuted with the $50 TV.

is stabbed four times by Henry off screen (the aural clues are linked to the earlier on-screen stabbing of the fence) and close-up shots of Henry's grimacing face are shown whilst he is stabbing the fence. The complexity of this murder made the scene very difficult for the BBFC to censor, as effectively the fence is killed in three different ways.

The scene is formally and thematically constructed in order to represent violence as entertainment. As such the scene employs various formal devices and strategies, including performance, dialogue, shot selection, editing, music and sound effects, in an attempt to foreground generic stylization and comedy over realism and authenticity. In terms of performance, during the first part of the scene Otis takes the lead in negotiations with the fence, whilst Henry stands by expressionless until the situation starts to spiral out of control. The fence's performance begins as sarcastic and humorous before becoming increasingly verbally aggressive.

Dramatic tension is built up in the scene by the way in which it is filmed and edited. The scene is shot using a range of static camera angles and from an objective point of view. As the scene develops, there are seven medium shots of Henry and Otis and eight medium close-ups of the fence; there then follows an increasing number of close-ups which emphasize the violent action but also remove it from its context: for example, an extreme close-up of the fence's hand being stabbed with the soldering iron and three close-ups of Henry's grimacing face as he repeatedly stabs the fence. Balance is maintained with two long shots of the three men struggling and two medium close-ups of Otis and the fence grappling, but emphasis is firmly placed upon the violent action toward the end of the scene. It thus adopts the conventional formal logic of close-ups serving to increase tension and long shots to relieve tension. In terms of editing, shot duration decreases as the violent action increases, adding a kinetic energy and dynamic rhythm to the scene. For example, the twenty shots leading up to the start of the physical violence against the fence last 143 seconds, giving an average shot duration of 7.15 seconds. The shift in rhythm precipitated by the onset of the physical violence is represented by thirteen shots lasting forty-eight seconds, with an

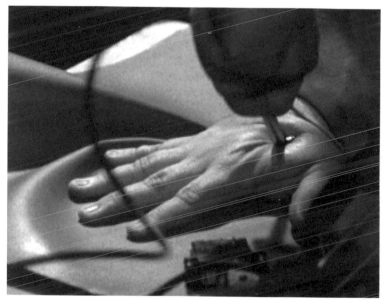

An extreme close-up of violent detail signalling a formal and temporal shift in the scene.

average shot duration of 3.67 seconds. Again, the scene thus conforms to a conventional formal logic of short, quick shots rapidly edited in order to increase the tension and pace of a violent scene.

With respect to sound, the scene draws upon a range of diegetic and non-diegetic aural signifiers, which are blended into the sound mix. These are stylized and generically coded, helping to make the violence more palatable and even pleasurable whilst simultaneously increasing the dramatic importance and affective impact of the scene. Before this point, the soundtrack accompanying the scene had been dominated by dialogue and diegetic sound effects (namely footsteps and the buzz of the TV being turned on); there is no music during the first part of the scene. The abrupt introduction of dramatic sound effects and music when the violence begins draws attention to the highly stylized nature of that violence thus detracting from its realism. For example, Henry's stabbing of the fence is accompanied by dramatic music and the high-pitched, synthesized sound effect of a dentist's drill, which is layered into the sound mix. As the TV is smashed over the fence's head, the accompanying dramatic music is replaced momentarily by the diegetic sound effect of the impact of the TV. Then sound effects linked to the fence's electrocution are foregrounded before the song 'Psycho' is introduced, which acts as a sound bridge to the next scene. The name of the track also adds extratextual resonance.

Home Invasion

The home-invasion scene takes place fifty-four minutes and three seconds into the film, and the sequence under examination lasts three minutes and sixteen seconds. The sequence has been selected because it has been consistently flagged up as the most controversial in the film. As Cettl suggests, 'it implicates the audience as complicit in murder in their viewing of the homemade snuff film, with the serial killer as director and actor' (2003, p. 205).

As noted earlier, in the UK the scene was cut from all versions of the film released between 1991 and 2003. The scene has also been selected because of its centrality within *Henry*'s mode of narratively orchestrating its violent attractions, signalling the crescendo of the film's violent spectacle and registering a key shift away from the slow revelation of that spectacle characteristic of its earlier scenes. In Freeland's view (1995), the film's violent spectacle eventually climaxes during the murder of Otis, and structural symmetry is restored at the end through the anti-climactic and off-screen murder of Becky.

Just before the scene, Henry and Otis are seen driving slowly along a suburban street at night. They turn right and stop outside a house. The soundtrack accompanying this sequence is a mix of non-diegetic dramatic music and non-diegetic sound effects consisting of distorted dialogue. The harsh sound mix draws attention to itself as a non-diegetic framing device and works against the realism implied by the actual physical location and the minimal lighting of the scene. Henry and Otis break into the house, an anonymous, middle-class, suburban family home, where they murder the son and husband and sexually assault and murder the wife, recording the events on a video camera stolen from the fence earlier. Towards the end of the scene it is revealed that the viewer is not witnessing the events in real time, but is in fact watching Henry and Otis's home-made 'snuff movie' on their TV back in Otis's apartment, after the event, and with the killers. The scene then cuts to Becky on the phone to her mother in the beauty parlour where she works. The scene is only partly contextualized by the initial approach to the house and by Henry and Otis's conversations about how to avoid police detection by varying their *modus operandi* and by keeping moving. In this sense, then, it does not involve a conventional build-up of suspense to its considerable violence.

The home-invasion scene formally and thematically constructs fictional violence that can be read as illegitimate, unjustified and unacceptable even within the serial-killer or horror film. The characters who make up the murdered family, whilst anonymous and featuring in the narrative only during this one scene, are constructed as illegitimate targets for violence. This is despite the fact that, as in the case of the fence, audiences have no knowledge of the family members compared with their knowledge of Henry and Otis. Whilst recognizing that the development of character relationships is fluid and can shift even within scenes, and that Henry and Otis are the narrative centres of the film, morally our sympathies lie more directly with the family.

This is the result of several interrelated factors. First, the assault on the family is represented as random, unprovoked and unpreventable; the house appears to have been simply stumbled upon and the invasion could have happened to any family. Second, the nuclear family is conventionally seen as a central pillar of western capitalist society and ideology, and consequently any attack on this institution is often considered unjustified and an attack on widely held values. Moreover, the father is shown to be powerless to prevent the abuse and murder of his wife, son and ultimately himself, thus undermining the patriarchal notion of the strong male head of the family – a key pillar of familial ideology. Third, any intrusion into a home is an invasion of private space and private property and, as such, appears even less acceptable than violence that takes place in public spaces, or in private spaces largely associated with criminality. Fourth, the family at the heart of the scene is relatively affluent, living in the suburbs and consequently unlikely to come into contact with working-class criminals. In this way too the family comes across as an unacceptable target, as the killers are completely out of place in this kind of social milieu. Fifth, the killing of the family involves the killing of a boy and his mother. In films it is often seen as ideologically and morally legitimate for bad men to kill each other, but children and their mothers are not legitimate targets, particularly if they are blameless. Sixth, the degree of physical abuse and specifically sexual humiliation experienced by the mother, especially in comparison to the treatment of the male members of the family, can be read as misogynistic and unacceptable. Seventh, the abuse of the dead mother's body and attempted necrophilia by Otis also test the boundaries of the audience. Eighth, implicating us in watching the violence as entertainment alongside the film-makers Henry and Otis, when we thought we were watching the home invasion happen in real time, is deliberately and effectively alienating.

The violence in this scene is framed by an operative modality that emphasizes seriousness and proximity to the real world and employs 'turn off', 'strong' and 'authentic' representations of violence. According to King (2004), the affective impact of film violence can be increased by deployment of two overlapping formal and thematic devices that can construct a serious modality. This scene illustrates the use of both: formal procedures linked to creating the impression of authenticity, directness and realism; and the playing down of overtly aesthetic, stylized qualities. These factors in combination connote that the violence within the scene should be taken seriously and not viewed as entertainment. 'Turn off' violence aims to portray violence within the moral framings of everyday life, emphasizing unpleasantness and disturbance, causing distress for viewers and problems for regulators (Corner, 1998).

'Strong' violence is characterized by depth of meaning, serves a narrative purpose and encourages emotional and moral responses in the spectator (McKinney, 1993). Similarly, 'authentic' violence can assault the sensibilities of those who watch it (Morrison *et al.*, 1999). Applied to this scene, these various considerations suggest that its violence breaks social and/or individual boundaries of moral acceptability, which is compounded by the fact that the violence looks realistic, is set within a domestic context and utilizes widely accessible weapons and recording technologies.

The scene represents explicitly several acts of on-screen and off-screen violence. The majority of on-screen violence, physical and sexual abuse and humiliation is directed at the mother by Otis. The violence against the son and father carried out by Henry occurs both on and off screen but does not involve explicit sexual abuse. During the scene, the mother is seen struggling with Otis, her arms held behind her back. He then manoeuvres her to a chair where he rips open her blouse, pulls up her bra up to reveal her right breast and fondles it. Following this, he lifts her skirt and puts his hand down the front of her tights. The father is then seen writhing on his side on the floor, his arms bound behind his back and a white pillowcase over his head. Blood is visible on the white material around the mouth area and on his shirt. He is kicked once off screen before being kicked a second time on screen. Henry then puts his left foot on the husband's shoulder, rolling him onto his back whilst shouting at him to shut up.[31] Next, the mother is seen struggling with Otis, her arm held behind her back and her legs flailing. Otis has his hand placed around the top of her exposed tights before moving it up to fondle and then kiss her exposed right breast. The son then enters the room. Henry puts the camera down and grabs the boy, pushing him into the middle of the room and onto the floor. Henry breaks his neck on screen in front of the mother, who is held by Otis, his hand placed over her mouth. The struggle between Henry and the son takes place half on and half off screen, at the bottom of the frame. Otis is seen to break the mother's neck as the father kicks Henry from off screen. Henry removes a knife from his back pocket and opens it before moving off screen to stab the father five times. The stabbing is signified by the

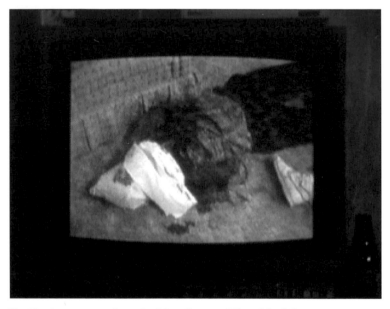

The bloody on-screen aftermath of the off-screen killing of the father.

aural cues of Henry's exertion, the knife impaling the father and his muffled cries of pain. Whilst the father is being killed off screen, Otis kisses the dead mother's mouth before fondling and then mauling her exposed breast. There is a shot of the dead father with a bloody pillowcase over his head and a very bloody chest. Blood is also visible on the carpet. The dead son is seen lying on the floor, his t-shirt lifted, head facing away from the camera with blood splatters on his chest. Otis then waves the dead mother's hand at the camera and moves her mouth as he says: 'Say bye, say hi' before waving her arm again. Otis then exposes and kisses her left breast and starts to remove her tights before being stopped by Henry. Back in their apartment, we see the video of the home invasion being rewound and then replayed in slow motion by Otis as the mother is again seen having her blouse ripped open and her bra pulled up, revealing her right breast as she struggles in anguish.

The first part of the scene, leading up to the revelation of the scene's conceit, employs a number of formal approaches and devices to create the impression of authenticity and a high level of realism. This impression of realism has been a major contributor to the controversy attached to *Henry*. Building upon the analysis outlined in the previous chapter, this section will now explore how this degree of realism is constructed by numerous approaches that are both formally and thematically motivated.

First, the scene rejects expensive production processes. Michael Rooker stood in for Charlie Lieberman as cameraman, using a Sony Betamax home video camera to capture the home invasion. At the point where Rooker steps from behind the camera it was returned to Lieberman, who positioned the camera on a cushion at a canted angle until Rooker returned to pick up the camera and film the rest of the scene.

Second, it was shot using formal devices and representational codes and conventions normally associated with documentary film-making. The sequence was shot handheld in *vérité* style on video in one continuous take, producing raw imagery with no music and only sparse dialogue. The start of the scene is shot from the subjective point of view of Henry, who is surveying the room through the viewfinder. The movement of the camera is erratic and jerky as Henry tries to capture the action. The framing of the shot stabilizes when filming Otis and the mother struggling, retaining a consistent medium shot.

Henry's reflection in wall mirrors behind the struggling Otis and the mother is also glimpsed several times during the scene. The soundtrack accompanying the sequence is devoid of music and dominated by the voices of Henry and Otis and the muffled screams of the mother, father and son. In terms of dialogue, Henry starts off the sequence, directing the action, with calls of 'Do it, Otis, you're a star' and 'You got it. Go for it, boy!' When the son enters the room, Henry puts the video camera on its side on the floor, and thus the next part of the scene is filmed at an angle, creating an even greater sense of unease; this is further compounded by the fact that some of the action is taking place off screen. At this point Henry moves from director to star of his

Henry clearly visible as the director of his and Otis's home-made 'snuff movie'.

'snuff movie' as he steps in front of the camera to kill the son and husband. After the murder of the father and son, Henry picks up the camera again and continues to film the events and aftermath from his point of view. Diegetic sound effects are layered into the mix, including the sound of the father being kicked twice, the camera being put on the floor, the son and mother having their necks broken, the heavy breathing of Henry after struggling with the son, the father being repeatedly stabbed and the video camera being picked up again. Once Otis starts to remove the dead mother's clothes, Henry intervenes shouting: 'Otis. No, Otis! Otis. … No!!'

The third way in which this sequence creates its impression of verisimilitude concerns the performative realism of its key actors. This is manifest in the casting of unknown actors and crew members to play the family and by constructing the set to be both as 'charged' and as natural as possible (Gregory, 2005).[32] The juxtaposition of the performances of Henry and Otis against the terror and desperate struggling of the mother, son and father further underlines the manner in which the realism of the scene is heightened by the perceived authenticity of the performances.

The second part of the scene reverts back to the film's more conventional approach to storytelling, including filming in 16mm and enlisting continuity editing and dramatic music. The main feature of this second part is the use of the distanciation device of drawing our attention to our complicity in the actions of Henry and Otis during the home invasion. This device works to reveal that we have not been witnessing the event unfold in real time but, rather, that we have been watching a pre-recorded 'snuff movie' alongside Henry and Otis in their apartment some time after the actual event itself. Formally and thematically positioning us alongside Henry and Otis as they watch their violence as entertainment potentially heightens the affective qualities of the scene whilst simultaneously distancing us from it. This then leads us to question what point the film-makers are trying to make in this particular scene, or the film in general, and to question how we feel, having sat through the home invasion.

The second part of the scene starts with the camera tracking left to right and moves in on Henry and Otis as they watch the home invasion on a stolen TV. The now non-diegetic sounds of Henry and Otis leaving the suburban home act as a sound bridge between the two parts of the scene before the diegetic sound effect of the video recorder being rewound is heard as Otis touches the remote control. The camera comes to a halt with Henry and Otis in a medium shot, and Henry asks Otis: 'What are you doing?' to which he replies: 'I want to see it again.' The film then cuts to the TV screen, with the video of the home invasion rewinding and then playing in slow motion. This is accompanied by the diegetic sound effect of the video on frame advance. A few seconds later, dramatic, non-diegetic music, distorted lines of dialogue and screams are introduced into the sound mix as the video plays in slow motion. There is then a cut to Otis smiling as he watches the film playing in slow motion on the TV, and Henry looking at him with displeasure. The camera tracks from right to left back towards the TV and

Henry looks disapprovingly at Otis as he rewinds the 'snuff movie' to watch it again.

then in on the TV until it dominates the frame, once more playing the early part of the home-invasion video in slow motion. The shot freezes on an image of Otis looking directly out of the screen having pulled the mother's bra up and over her breasts. The screen fades to black and then dissolves into a shot of Becky on the phone to her mother in the beauty parlour where she works.

Formally, the conceit of audience complicity revealed during the second part of the home-invasion scene is framed diegetically by the earlier scene in which Henry, Otis and Becky make a home video with the equipment stolen after the murder of the fence. During this earlier scene we see, on the screen of the stolen TV, images of Henry and Becky dancing as they are filmed in real time by Otis. The frame of the stolen TV set acts as a frame within the frame of the film. The home-invasion scene is presented using the same frame-within-a-frame device, helping to create the impression that we are watching the images in real time rather than in video playback. This narrative, formal

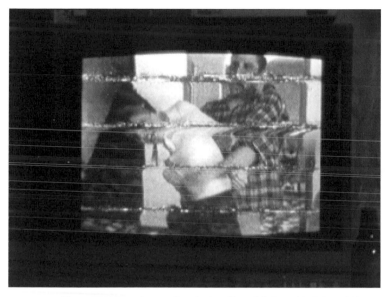

Viewers are forced to re-view the 'snuff movie' alongside Otis and Henry.

and thematic bridging of a number of scenes in the film with and through video technology has been read as reflecting a critique of the technologies of representation within contemporary postmodern culture.

The home-invasion scene's recourse to a number of formal approaches and devices to create an impression of authenticity also makes it anything but 'entertaining' in the conventional sense of the word. As noted in the analysis of audience responses to *Henry* outlined in the preceding chapter, this sequence has the very strong potential narratively and ideologically to shock and alienate viewers. Over time that shock has become a cultural phenomenon, epitomizing the controversy around the film and framing its legacy (Readman, 2005). For example, the research carried out by Hill (1997) found that *Henry* was not generally seen as entertaining because of what participants perceived as its documentary realism, which aligned its fictional violence uncomfortably closely with real-life violence, making the film all the more

The framing of an earlier scene helps to shape our reading of the home invasion.

disturbing and challenging through the removal of the distancing features of fictional violence, such as stylization. Hill's participants reported that they did not allow themselves to become involved directly and deeply with material of this nature because it was perceived to be too close to real-life events and, as such, was too painful, unsettling and potentially shocking for them. This sequence was recognized as particularly testing because of the way in which it provoked personal responses to wider social thresholds and taboos. For example, as noted earlier, Hill's participants cited sexual violence, violence against children and the use of everyday weapons, such as knives, in interpersonal violence as being particularly disturbing. However, an obvious irony here is that responses such as these overlook the artifice that has gone into *creating* this impression of realism, which, whilst attempting to *break down* the distance between film and viewer, involves as much construction and artifice as those stylized forms of film violence, which are seen as more entertaining because of the safe distance which they *establish* between film and viewer.

Whilst acknowledging the challenge of applying categories of violence with any consistency and precision, Corner (1998) highlights how certain films employ in their basic design a shift from 'turn on' to 'turn off' violence, or *vice versa*, which often gives rise to debate over their moral ambivalence. King (2004) also highlights how the balance of operative modalities in a film can change from moment to moment, and indeed *Henry* contains several self-conscious shifts in its representation of violence, from 'turn on' and 'weak' violence in the 'shopping' scene to 'turn off', 'strong' and 'authentic' violence' in the home invasion. The scenes have also been constructed formally and thematically so as to utilize very different mixes of modality in their representations of violence.

As a result, the violent scenes can be read relationally through a number of binary oppositions including: legitimate and illegitimate; justified and unjustified; acceptable and unacceptable; innocent and guilty; comedic and serious; surface meaning and deep meaning; narrative purpose and no narrative purpose; pleasure and displeasure; entertaining and not entertaining; emotional engagement and no emotional engagement; moral response and no moral response; conservative and challenging; conventional suspense set-up and no suspense set-up; upsetting and not upsetting; common and rare; formalist style and realist style; horror film and 'snuff movie'. In *Henry*, the relationship between the scenes of violence, and especially the juxtaposition of these scenes, have the potential greatly to increase the affective qualities of the home-invasion scene. This is because, up to that point, by withholding violent spectacle (via the use of tableaux) and then showing violent spectacle ameliorated by stylization, generic codes and comedy (the 'shopping' scene), the film has set up certain expectations, expectations that the home-invasion scene deliberately and provocatively breaches.

McNaughton has suggested that his intention in the 'shopping' scene was to reflect the dominant Hollywood paradigm of presenting violence as entertaining, gratifying and cathartic:

> One of the big themes in *Henry* is violence as entertainment. Normally, the way you develop the theme is to set up a character to be a bad guy … and then turn up the heat where you dislike him enough that you are happy to see one of the heroes slaughter him. And you get a cathartic release. That's sort of what we did. In the scene with the television set, here's this big, fat, ugly guy … . We did everything we could to make him distasteful and repulsive … . 'Here's violence for entertainment the way you like it, folks!' (quoted in Falsetto, 2000, p. 328)

By contrast, his objective in the home-invasion scene was to implicate film-makers and audiences within the narrative and to raise questions about watching film violence as entertainment:

> Okay wasn't that a lot of fun? [The 'shopping' scene]. Now, we're going to show you what it might look like to move in on an innocent family and just slaughter them randomly. It's about as ugly a thing as you're ever likely to see. 'Now how much fun was that?' To take the audience one way, and then show them what it might really be like. And then we pulled a double trick of going in the house and seeing that they've got a camera … . You think you are still in the room with them but, indeed, you're seeing the playback later on a TV screen, and they're now entertaining themselves with the record of their own mayhem. And you're sitting right next to them in a kind of complicity. (quoted in ibid.)

However, this meta-fictional assertion has itself proved extremely contentious with critics, academics, audiences and regulators. But whatever the case, in this context it is surely significant that, in the UK, the 'shopping' scene did not attract anything like the same level of criticism for being 'too violent' as did the home-invasion scene, the former losing only four seconds of process violence from the film's 1993 video release, whilst the latter was variously cut and rearranged by the BBFC before finally being allowed through the censorship process in its entirety. And it is also notable that, although the home-invasion scene is almost universally singled out as the film's most controversial moment, the climax of *Henry*'s gradually intensifying spectacle actually comes with the intense, brutal and sexualized murder of Otis.

This chapter has focused on the textual analysis of three scenes that have been recognized in academic, fan, critical and regulatory discourses as being central to the controversy surrounding *Henry*. It has been suggested that the scenes fit into *Henry*'s particular mode of narratively orchestrating its violent attractions, which consists in the slow revelation of violent spectacle before concealing it again during the film's anticlimax. The chapter has also examined the overlapping incorporation of various potentially distancing devices, the mixing of modalities in the representation of violence and the juxtaposing of different categories of film violence. As a consequence of the employment of these strategies, *Henry* can be understood to have exploited rather than simply employed film violence: it is this which has provoked so many divergent opinions about (and prompted meta-textual reflection upon) the representation of violence, not simply in this film but in films in general. According to King, 'a balance is usually found between the intense orchestration of violence and legitimating frameworks that make it palatable for both audiences and regulatory authorities' (2004, p. 129). It is precisely *Henry*'s destabilization of this equilibrium that is the major factor in the creation and maintenance of the controversy that still attaches to the film.

✖ PART 5

THE LEGACY OF *HENRY: PORTRAIT OF A SERIAL KILLER*

The aim of this conclusion is twofold. First, it will offer a summary of the main factors contributing to the controversy surrounding *Henry* and in so doing will offer a model which, whilst specific to this case study, could serve as a starting point for the analysis of other controversial films. Second, it will reflect upon the unfolding legacy of *Henry* within a range of distinct but related contexts.

Modelling Controversy

Henry has been controversial for so long and across several territories due to numerous intentional and unintentional factors. These include the overlapping contexts (political, social, cultural, economic, industrial and technological) within which *Henry* was produced, regulated, distributed, exhibited and consumed; the film-maker's vision, which set out deliberately to remove the buffer of fantasy by looking at the everyday life of a serial killer without offering reasons or justifications for his actions, refusing to judge him or to offer any final redemption or resolution; its curious status as a fictionalized account of the story of a real person, Henry Lee Lucas, partly based on confessions that he later retracted; and its production history, which, for various aesthetic, industrial and budgetary reasons, drew upon techniques connoting authenticity and realism whilst also employing various stylized formal devices. *Henry* was an exercise in 'purposeful confusion' and 'instability', setting up a number of tensions and contradictions without sorting them out; it also fell uncomfortably between the cracks of several different film-making traditions and genres, making the film difficult to interpret and respond to. Finally, whilst it was contained within mainstream formal and narrative codes and conventions, *Henry* also diverged from them sufficiently to alienate certain audiences.

Further factors that have helped to fuel the ongoing debate about the film include: *Henry*'s thematic provocations with respect to its ambiguous representations of power, class, gender, sexuality and ethnicity, all of which worked both within and against generic conventions; its fictional representations of violence, which, within its mode of narrative orchestration of violent attractions, pose a range of meta-textual questions about film violence in general and about the way in which it is consumed; the manner in which it polarized critical, journalistic, audience and academic responses, which were characterized by a mixture of revulsion and admiration and which in turn formed constituting frameworks for the propagation and framing of subsequent controversy; its approach to publicity, advertising and marketing, which foregrounded that controversy, as well as its critical reception and markers of authenticity, as a means of selling the film; its testing of regulatory thresholds resulting from its lack of 'moral tone' in the US and its breaching of the Video Recordings Act in the UK, where initially it was heavily cut; the delay between the film's production, distribution, classification/censorship and consumption, which meant that it was a text slightly out of kilter with the various contexts in which it found itself; and its testing of audiences' thresholds and boundaries by the manner in which it required them actively to create meaning during the viewing experience itself.

Henry's Legacy

Despite initial claims that *Henry* was 'almost too widely acclaimed to be considered a cult film' (Rubin, 1992, p. 55), for many fans, critics and academics it has since gained precisely this reputation. Cult status is often conferred as the result of the recognition of particular 'networks of relationships' between text, context, circulation and reception (Mendik and Harper, 2000). However, the term 'cult' is notoriously difficult to define and apply because of the eclectic nature of the films to which it is all too often applied, the numerous different approaches brought to the subject, and the number of parties with an investment in the term (Jancovich *et al.*, 2003). *Henry* has been identified as a cult film for a variety of reasons linked to: text (formal, generic and narrative deviations from horror conventions); context (transgressive engagement with culture, politics and technology, resulting in various forms of censorship); circulation (a particular history of distribution, exhibition, marketing and promotion); and reception (audience engagement, critical reception and academic analysis). However, as discussed in Parts 3 and 4, *Henry*, whilst perceived by some as transgressive, is constrained by a wider range of counter-dynamics operating within the text (King, 2005, 2007). It can also be argued that the voices claiming cult status for *Henry* are often those of white, middle-class males attempting to legitimate their specific masculine dispositions (Jancovich *et al.*, 2003, p. 2) or their elite cinephilia (Sconce, 1993, pp. 104–5) and helping to maintain a distinction between 'masculine' cult films and a 'feminized' mainstream (Hollows, 2003, p. 37).

In academic literature on horror and serial-killer cinema, *Henry*'s legacy is actually somewhat marginal, and often splits authors along theoretical divides. Those for whom serial killers are a product of modernity (and especially the alienating forces of capitalist production and increased social mobility) can be critical of *Henry* for its lack of moral orientation and/or for its problematic ideological orientation towards questions of power, class, gender, sexuality and ethnicity. Meanwhile, others who actually share some of these concerns argue that *Henry*, through its formal and narrative logic, is able to distance audiences from its subject matter and thus to encourage them to question the role of the serial killer, film violence and power relations within society.[33] Authors who believe that serial killers are a manifestation of postmodernity (characterized by fragmentation, simulation and distrust of meta-narratives) are frequently supportive of *Henry* for its refusal to attempt to explain multiple murderers and its critique of technologies of representation.[34]

Henry's legacy is also significant in more popular writings about film, in which it is often cited as a cornerstone of contemporary horror cinema. *Henry* often features in lists of the best or most scary horror films, including

Entertainment Weekly's '20 Most Scary Movies of All Time' (Ascher-Walsh *et al.*, 2004) and *101 Horror Films You Must See before You Die* (Schneider, 2009). The 'Henry Theme' also features on several horror soundtrack compilation albums including *The Sound of Horror and Thriller* (2008). *Henry* is often positioned with, but not necessarily directly alongside, a group of other independent American films shot on small budgets by directors in the early stages of their film careers who sought to revitalize the horror genre in their respective decades: for example, *Night of the Living Dead* (1968), *The Last House on the Left* (1972), *Halloween*, *The Evil Dead* (1981) and *The Blair Witch Project* (1999). Because of the delay between production and circulation, *Henry* is often referred to in association with either a range of films characterized as the 'new brutalism' or with bigger-budget, mainstream, serial-killer movies such as *The Silence of the Lambs*. *Henry* is also cited alongside some other films that create a particularly affective tone, including *The Texas Chainsaw Massacre*, *Maniac*, *Seul contre tous/I Stand Alone* (1998) and *Irréversible* (2002). However, it is rare for books to devote whole chapters to *Henry*, references to it tending to occur in the intertextual context of discussion of horror or serial-killer films or in analyses of US independent cinema, film narrative and form, or in discussions of film violence.[35] This is the first book-length treatment of the film.

The legacy of *Henry* also lives on in fan discourse and activity. During the research for this book, references to Henry were found on a wide variety of online fan and review sites. IMDB user comments for *Henry* amounted to 177 posts, with 75 indicating that they loved it and 43 that they hated it (IMDB, 2011).[36] As of February 2011 the IMDB user rating for *Henry* is 7.2 out of 10 with 10,128 votes.[37] Ebay is a popular place for people to trade copies of the film, soundtracks and publicity materials. YouTube boasts multiple links including film trailers, extracts from the film, fan reviews, extracts from interviews at conventions and parodies of key scenes, including the short film *Henry and Becky*.[38]

Henry's legacy can be seen directly and indirectly in a number of films that structure themselves around what Simpson (2000) calls 'psycho profile' and 'masculine hero' serial-killer films, including: *Henry 2*, *Schramm* (1993), *Nutbag* (2000), *Roberto Succo* (2001), *H6: Diary of a Serial Killer* (2004), *Murder Set Pieces* (2004) and *Tony* (2009). *Henry*'s influence can also be seen in films based around actual serial killers, including *Ed Gein*, *Dahmer* (2002), *Bundy* (2002), *Gacy* (2003), *Monster* (2003) and *Henry Lee Lucas: Serial Killer*.[39] The legacy of *Henry* can be identified less directly in films that engage with similar formal and thematic concerns, such as meta-fictional reflections on the watching of film violence, the use within a film of self-made 'snuff movies' utilizing the latest technologies, or audiences' complicity with screen violence. For example, *Man Bites Dog*, *Funny Games* (1997, 2008), *The Last Horror Movie* (2003) and *Eden Lake* (2008), in which the acts of brutality are recorded on a mobile phone, the recordings becoming a major plot device as the film unfolds.

The legacy of *Henry* can also be witnessed in less direct and more ironic postmodern intertextual lenses in films such as *Serial Mom* and McNaughton's second film *The Borrower*, in which *Henry* is actually referred to several times. In Nanni Moretti's *Caro diario/Dear Diary* (1993) the director goes into a cinema in Rome to watch *Henry* and is so disgusted that he imagines visiting an Italian journalist, reading him his review of the film, and satirizing his postmodern defence of it. Michael Rooker relived his Henry persona in the music video *All Wrapped Up*, made by industrial metal band American Head Charge.[40] The heavy metal band Jag Panzer featured the song track 'GMV 407'[41] on their 1994 album *Dissent Alliance*, whilst Fantômas performed an interpretation of the 'Henry Theme' entitled *Henry: Portrait of a Serial Killer* on their 2001 album *The Director's Cut*.

Henry also lives on in marketing and advertising discourses often linked to the critical reception of more contemporary films. For example, the backcover of the Barrel Entertainment release of *Schramm* contains the quote 'One of the creepiest portraits since *Henry: Portrait of a Serial Killer*' – from *Shock Cinema*, whilst the frontcover of the UK DVD release of *The Last Horror Movie* has: 'Stomps in the footprints set by *Henry: Portrait of a Serial Killer*' from *Hotdog*. In a more recent example, the backcover of the US DVD

A self-reflexive reference to *Henry* in *The Borrower*.

release of the *The Girl Next Door* (2007) quotes Stephen King thus: 'The first authentically shocking American film I've seen since *Henry: Portrait of a Serial Killer* over 20 years ago.' Moreover, the backcover of the UK DVD release of *Tony* states: 'The outstanding debut from Gerard Johnson, *Tony* has been compared to classics *Henry: Portrait of a Serial Killer* and *Taxi Driver* and is one of the most important and disturbing British films of recent years.' These examples reveal how the legacy of *Henry* still frames the writings of reviewers and journalists and how these links are drawn upon by distributors and marketers in order to help position and sell their films within the horror marketplace.

Finally, a further two points linked to *Henry*'s ongoing legacy need to be noted. First, during the research for this book my request to the BBFC to look at their files on *Henry* was denied. This is because it operates a system whereby any file which is less than twenty years' old is not accessible for public inspection. The BBFC argued that, whilst *Henry* was produced in 1986, it was not submitted to the Board until 1990 and not classified for theatrical release until July 1991. As a result, the files for *Henry* would not be available for public access until 2011, which was after the deadline for the manuscript of this book. This means that, despite the BBFC becoming more open and accountable in recent years, a full examination of *Henry*'s UK regulatory journey will have to wait. Second, on 16 August 2008 *Henry* was screened at 'Terror in the Aisles', a festival held in Chicago, at which McNaughton was invited to give a Q&A. Online reports suggested that McNaughton declined to talk about *Henry* during the Q&A and then raced off after the event, refusing to speak to fans or to do any signing. This is illustrative of a fundamental aspect of *Henry*'s legacy, namely that, despite a successful subsequent career, McNaughton will always be associated with the film, a situation that for him is distinctly double-edged. *Henry* was the springboard that launched McNaughton into the industry, but the controversy that it created, whether he likes it or not, continues to define his career.

✕ APPENDICES

Appendix A: Key Details

Cast (In Order of Appearance)

Dead Woman	Mary Demas	Woman in Cadillac	Flo Spink
Henry	Michael Rooker	High-school Jock	Kurt Naebig
Waitress	Anne Bartoletti	Hooker 1	Mary Demas
Dead Couple (Wife)	Elizabeth Kaden	Hooker 2	Kristin Finger
Dead Couple (Husband)	Ted Kaden	Woman in Beauty Shop	Lily Monkus
Dead Prostitute	Mary Demas	Fence	Ray Atherton
Floating Woman	Denise Sullivan	Parole Officer	Eric Young
Mall Shopper 1	Anita Ores	Shooting Victim	Rick Paul
Mall Shopper 2	Megan Ores	Bum 1	Peter Van Wagner
Mall Shopper 3	Cheri Jones	Bum 2	Tom McKearn
Mall Victim	Monica Anne O'Malley	Bum 3	Frank Coronado
Husband	Bruce Quist	Murdered Family – Wife	Lisa Temple
Hitch-hiker	Erzsebet Sziky	Murdered Family – Husband	Brian Graham
Becky	Tracy Arnold	Murdered Family – Son	Sean Ores
Otis	Tom Towles	Hair Stylist	Pamela Fox
Henry's Boss	David Katz	Store Clerk	Waleed B. Ali
Kid with Football 1	John Scafidi	Dog Walker	Donna Dunlap
Kid with Football 2	Benjamen Passman	Delores	Augie the Dog

Production Crew

Director	John McNaughton	Editing	Elena Maganini
Art Direction	Rick Paul	Director of Photography	Charlie Lieberman
Costumes	Patricia Hart	Executive Producers	Waleed B. Ali
Music	Robert McNaughton		Malik B. Ali
	Ken Hale	Script	Richard Fire
	Steven A. Jones		John McNaughton

Producers	John McNaughton	Sound Effects	Dan Haberkorn
	Lisa Dedmond	Post-production	Ric Coken
	Steven A. Jones	Sound Mixers	Elena Maganini
Production Manager	Lisa Dedmond	Assistant Post-	Louie Quiroz
Sound Recordist	Thomas T. Yore	production Sound Mixer	
First Assistant Director	Paul Chen	Music Recording	Tone Zone
Second Assistant	Andrew Bradburn		Recording, Chicago
Director		Post-production Sound	Zenith DB, Chicago
Script Supervisor	Melanie Hecht	Services	
Make-up Artist	Berndt Rantscheff	Casting	Jeffrey Lyle Segal
Special Effects	Jeffrey Lyle Segal	Storyboard Artist	Frank Coronado
Make-up		Acting Coach	Richard Fire
Make-up Effects Crew	Michael J. Alonzi	Fight Co-ordinator	David Wooley
	Scott Whitehead	Still Photographers	Paul Petraitis
	Herb Nordheimer		Berndt Rantscheff
Technical Effects	Lee Ditkowski	Catering	Sprout Route Ltd
Set Dressing and Props	Rick Paul	Title Design	Steven A. Jones
Wardrobe	Patricia Hart		David LeBoy
Hair Stylist	Chuck Gatz	Excerpts from *Becket*	Courtesy MPI Home
Grips	Dave Buckley	(1964)	Video
	Brian Graham	Film Processing	Allied Film Labs,
Camera Assistants	Dave Mahlman		Chicago
	Brad Sellars	Music Director	Steven A. Jones
Production Assistant	Bradley Magon	Soundtrack Publisher	Alloy Music ASCAP
Post-production	Steven A. Jones	Production Company	Maljack Productions
Supervisor			

Appendix B: Release, Business and Awards Details

Alternative Titles

Henry – Portrait d'un tueur	Canada (French title)
Henry – en massmördare	Sweden
Henry – pioggia di sangue	Italy
Henry Lee Lucas – sarjamurhaaja	Finland
Henry, portrait d'un serial killer	France
Henry, retrat d'un assassí	Spain (Catalan title)
Henry, retrato de un asesino	Spain
Henry, to portraito enos dolofonou	Greece
Henry: A Sombra de um assassino	Portugal
Henry: portret seryjnego zabójcy	Poland
Retrato de um assassino	Brazil

Business

Budget	$111,000 (estimated)
US box-office gross	$609,939
UK box-office gross	£72,589
UK video retail figures	£6,894 (Electric Pictures, August 1996)

Locations

Austin, Texas, USA
Chicago, Illinois, USA

Awards and Nominations

Michael Rooker, Golden Space Needle, Best Actor, Seattle International Film Festival, June 1990.

John McNaughton, nominated for Golden Leopard, Locarno International Film Festival, August 1990.

John McNaughton, Best Director, (tied with Sam Raimi for *Darkman*), Sitges – Catalonian International Film Festival, October 1990.

John McNaughton, Best Film, Sitges – Catalonian International Film Festival, October 1990.

John McNaughton, Prize of the Catalan Screenwriters', Critics' and Writers' Association at Sitges, Catalonian International Film Festival, October 1990.

John McNaughton, International Fantasy Film Award, Best Film, Fantasporto, February 1991.

Richard Fire and John McNaughton, International Fantasy Film Award, Best Screenplay, Fantasporto, February 1991.

Michael Rooker, International Fantasy Film Award, Best Actor, Fantasporto, February 1991.

Tracy Arnold, International Fantasy Film Award, Best Actress (tied with Billie Whitelaw for *The Krays*), Fantasporto, February 1991.

John McNaughton, Silver Raven, Brussels International Festival of Fantasy Film, March 1991.

John McNaughton, nominated for Best Director, Independent Spirit Awards, March 1991.

John McNaughton, Lisa Dedmond and Steven A. Jones, nominated for Best Feature, Independent Spirit Awards, March 1991.

Michael Rooker, nominated for Best Lead Male, Independent Spirit Awards, March 1991.

John McNaughton and Richard Fire, nominated for Best Screenplay, Independent Spirit Awards, March 1991.

Tracy Arnold, nominated for Best Supporting Female, Independent Spirit Awards, March 1991.

Tom Towles, nominated for Best Supporting Male, Independent Spirit Awards, March 1991.

Appendix C: Notes

1 The original title was *Henry* but the film's producers changed it to *Henry: Portrait of a Serial Killer* to distinguish it from other '*Henry*'s available on video.

2 'Henry' is used here to refer to the character of Henry in the film. 'Henry Lee Lucas' will be used to refer to the actual serial killer upon whom the film was loosely based.

3 Here film *regulation* is defined as the frameworks within which censorship and classification decisions are made and justified; film *censorship* as the process of re-editing, cutting or banning films; and film *classification* as the allocation of the age categories used to control access to films.

4 'Otis' is used here to refer to the character in the film. 'Ottis' will be used to refer to the actual serial killer upon whom the film is loosely based.

5 According to King (2005), during the mid-1980s the production costs of low-budget independent films were in the region of $500,000–$1,000,000 – making *Henry* an ultra low-budget film. This would later be an important factor in the critical reception and marketing of the movie.

6 Seventy-four of these storyboards can be found on the 20th Anniversary Special Edition.

7 McNaughton has suggested that this casting is metaphorical in that someone known for dealing in audiovisual software plays a character who deals in audiovisual hardware.

8 McNaughton has suggested that this casting, too, is also metaphorical in that one of the two financiers of *Henry* plays a character who runs a store.

9 McNaughton's commentaries (2003b; McNaughton and Gregory, 2005a) reflect on the fact that several of the locations used in *Henry* have, since 1985, become gentrified and sought-after areas in which to live.

10 These scenes with a commentary can be found on the 20th Anniversary Special Edition.

11 Vestron would go on to have production success with *Dirty Dancing* (1987) but go out of business in 1989 as a result of overstretching themselves by moving into production.

12 The Coleman image is available as a reversible cover on the 20th Anniversary Special Edition.

13 Like Vestron, Atlantic would go out of business by moving into production and becoming overstretched.

14 *Henry* was released theatrically in Canada by Cinépix Film Properties (CFP) during 1990. *Henry* was also screened at the Seattle International Film Festival in June, the Munich Film Festival in June/July, the Locarno International Film Festival in August 1990, and at Sitges in October. In 1991 it was screened at MILFED in Milan.

15 An extended version of this quote appears on the film poster of *Henry* circulating during its initial theatrical release, 'TWO THUMBS UP … *Henry* is a powerful and important film, brilliantly directed and acted' (Siskel and Ebert).

16 Quotes cited on film posters in circulation at the time of theatrical release.

17 In Europe *Henry* was released theatrically in France on 6 February 1991, in Spain on 10 April 1991, in Italy and Sweden on 24 July 1992, in Finland on 20 November 1992, and in the Netherlands on 8 April 1993. *Henry* was also released theatrically in Australia on 11 June 1993.

18 *The Silence of the Lambs* grossed $130 million dollars at the US box office and is the only horror film to have received five Oscars.

19 Although this edition does not appear on the BBFC database, the author has a copy of the laserdisc release in his possession (catalogue number E1002E, labelled as an '18' certificate).

20 The commodification of *Henry* can be traced back to the MPI US video release which, according to Jeffrey S. Pence (1994) carried advertisements for *Henry* t-shirts and posters.

21 At one point in the narrative, Henry tells Louisa that he contemplated committing suicide after the murders of his friends Becky and Otis, making a direct connection to *Henry*.

22 A similar cut can be found in the German '16' version of *Henry*.

23 It is noteworthy that at this time completely uncut versions of *Henry* were available in America, Germany and the Netherlands.

24 Research undertaken on behalf of the BBFC into the consumption of sexual violence by film viewers in the UK includes Cumberbatch *et al*. (2002) and Barker *et al*. (2007).

25 Ideological positions which McNaughton could be seen to be challenging in his oeuvre. As Falsetto suggests: 'McNaughton's own background growing up in south-side Chicago no doubt gave him insight into the plight of the working-class who were falling between the cracks in Ronald Reagan's conservative economic "revolution" in the 1980s' (2000, pp. 319–20).

26 Film form is taken to refer to a variety of textual features, including camera positioning, movement and framing, image quality and textures, sound and editing regimes (King, 2005).

27 Hill's target films included *Henry: Portrait of a Serial Killer*, *Reservoir Dogs*, *Man Bites Dog*, *True Romance*, *Pulp Fiction*, *Natural Born Killers* and *Killing Zoe*.

28 The quotations cited here were sampled from 177 IMDB user comments on *Henry*.

29 This particular version of *Henry* has been chosen for two reasons: it is an uncut version, and it has a subtitle track, making the analysis of dialogue easier.

30 This tableau has featured in all US versions of *Henry* released since 1990.

31 This line of dialogue is also used in the sound mix of the 'third tableau', thus acting as an aural device linking these scenes within the film's mode of narratively orchestrating its violent attractions.

32 Interviews with the actors in the DVD documentary *Portrait: The Making of Henry* reveal that the sequence was shot only twice, that during the filming Lisa Temple hurt her neck and that she was 'overwhelmed' by the way in which the sequence was approached and filmed.

33 For readings which work within these frameworks see Taubin (1991), Sconce (1993), Dyer (1993, 1997), Hantke (2001) and Hallam and Marshment (2000).

34 For postmodern readings of *Henry*, see Rubin (1992), Pence (1994), Freeland (1995), Pinedo (1997), Sharrett (1999) and Simpson (2000).

35 See Mathews (1994), Hardy (1997), Bouzereau (2000), Fuchs (2002), Kermode (2002), Armstrong (2003), Cettl (2003), Fullwood (2003), Marriott (2004) and Marriott and Newman (2006).

36 IMDB user comments posted between December 1998 and January 2011.

37 The votes break down into men: 7,031, women: 630. Most men were aged between eighteen and forty-four (18–28: 3,079 and 30–44: 379).

38 See http://www.youtube.com/watch?v=XSKPawe2_O8.

39 Some critics are keen to point out the distinction between *Henry* and the later, character-based films about actual serial killers, because of the perceived realism and authenticity of *Henry*.

40 The track features on the band's 2001 album *The Art of War*.

41 GMV 407 is the licence plate of the car that Henry drives in the film.

Appendix D: References

Abbott, H. Porter (2002) *The Cambridge Introduction to Narrative*. Cambridge: Cambridge University Press.

Andrews, Paul (2007) 'Decent but Dull Serial Killer Film', IMDB user reviews. Available from: http://www.imdb.com/title/tt0099763/usercomments?filter=chrono;start=20 [accessed 10 December 2008].

Armstrong, Kent Byron (2003) *Slasher Films: An International Filmography 1960 through 2001*. Jefferson, NC: McFarland.

Ascher-Walsh, R. *et al.* (2004) 'The 20 Scariest Movies of All Time'. Available from: http://www.ew.com/ew/article/0,,726267_5,00.html [accessed 23 April 2009].

ba.harrison (2007) 'Uncompromising, Brutal and Disturbing Film-making'. Available from: http://www.imdb.com/title/tt0099763/usercomments?filter=chrono;start=20 [accessed 15 December 2008].

Barker, Martin (1995) 'Violence', *Sight and Sound*, June 1995, pp. 10–13.

Barker, Martin (1997) 'The Newson Report: A Case Study in Common Sense' in Martin Barker and Julian Petley (eds) *Ill Effects: The Media/Violence Debate*. London: Routledge, pp.12–31.

Barker, Martin *et al.* (2007) *Audiences and Receptions of Sexual Violence in Contemporary Cinema*. London: British Board of Film Classification.

Bates, Peter (1990) 'Lost and Found', *Cineaste* vol. 17 no. 4, pp. 56–7.

BBFC (2007) *Henry Portrait of a Serial Killer*. Available from: http://www.bbfc.co.uk/website/classified.nsf/0/8D6625784CFAC93180256CD70027 [accessed 4 December 2007].

bob the moo (2007) 'Downbeat and Unpleasant Film That Is All the Better for It'. Available from: http://www.imdb.com/title/tt0099763/usercomments?filter=chrono;start=20 [accessed 19 December 2008].

Bouzereau, Laurent (2000) *Ultraviolent Movies: From Sam Peckinpah to Quentin Tarantino*, 2nd edn. New York: Citadel Press.

Carter, Cynthia and C. K. Weaver (2003) *Violence and the Media: Issues in Cultural and Media Studies*. Buckingham: Open University Press.

Cettl, Robert (2003) *Serial Killer Cinema: An Analytical Filmography with an Introduction*. Jefferson, NC: McFarland.

Charney, Leo (2001) 'The Violence of a Perfect Moment' in David J. Slocum (ed.) *Violence and American Cinema*. London: Routledge, pp. 47–62.

Cohen, Stanley (2002) *Folk Devils and Moral Panics*, 3rd edn. London: Routledge.

Corner, John (1998) 'Why Study Media Form?' in Adam Briggs and Paul Cobley (eds) *The Media: An Introduction*. Harlow: Longman, pp. 238–49.

Cornetarquin (2005) 'Sick Rubbish'. Available from: http://www.imdb.com/title/tt0099763/usercomments?filter=hate;start=0 [accessed 19 December 2008].

Cumberbatch, Guy *et al.* (2002) *Where Do You Draw the Line? Attitudes and Reactions of Video Renters to Sexual Violence in Film.* London: British Board of Film Classification.

dee.reid (2008) 'Downbeat and Unpleasant Film'. Available from: http://www.imdb.com/title/tt0099763/usercomments?filter=chrono;start=20 [accessed 10 December 2008].

Dyer, Richard (1993) *The Matter of Images: Essays on Representation*, 2nd edn. London: Routledge.

Dyer, Richard (1997) 'Kill and Kill Again', *Sight and Sound*, September 1997, pp. 4–17.

Ebert, Roger (1990) *'Henry: Portrait of a Serial Killer'*, *Chicago Sun-Times*, 14 September. Available from: http://rogerebert.suntimes.com/apps/pbcs.dll/article?AID=/19900914/REVIEWS/9140301/1023 [accessed 10 November 2007].

Falsetto, Mario (2000) *Personal Visions: Conversations with Contemporary Film Directors*. Los Angeles, CA: Silman-James Press.

Freeland, Cynthia A. (1995) 'Realist Horror' in Cynthia A. Freeland and Thomas E. Wartenberg (eds) *Philosophy and Film*. London: Routledge, pp. 126–42.

Freeland, Cynthia A. (2009) *'Henry: Portrait of a Serial Killer'* in Steven Jay Schneider (ed.) *1001 Movies You Must See before You Die*. London: Cassell, pp. 312–15.

Fuchs, Cynthia (2002) *Bad Blood: An Illustrated Guide to Psycho Cinema Inspired by 20th Century Serial Killers and Murderers*. London: Creation Books.

Fullwood, Neil (2003) *One Hundred Violent Films That Changed Cinema*. London: Batsford.

Gregory, David (2005) 'Portrait: The Making of *Henry*', supplementary material on the 20th Anniversary Special Edition DVD of *Henry: Portrait of a Serial Killer*. Orland Park, IL: Dark Sky Films.

Hallam, Julia and Margaret Marshment (2000) *Realism and Popular Cinema*. Manchester: Manchester University Press.

Hantke, Steffen (2001) 'Violence Incorporated: John McNaughton's *Henry: Portrait of a Serial Killer* and the Uses of Gratuitous Violence in Popular Narrative', *College Literature* vol. 28 no. 2, pp. 29–47.

Harbord, Janet (2002) *Film Cultures*. London: Sage.

Hardy, Phil (ed.) (1997) *The BFI Companion to Crime*. London: Cassell/BFI.

Hendershot, Heather (1998) *Saturday Morning Censors: Television Regulation before the V-Chip*. Durham, NC: Duke University Press.

Hill, Annette (1997) *Shocking Entertainment: Viewer Responses to Violent Movies*. Luton: John Libbey.

Hollows, Joanne (2003) 'The Masculinity of Cult' in Mark Jancovich, Antonio Lazaro Reboll, Julian Stringer and Andrew Willis (eds) *Defining Cult Movies: The Cultural Politics of Oppositional Taste*. Manchester: Manchester University Press.

IMDB (2011) User Comments. Available from: http://www.imdb.com/title/tt0099763/usercomments [accessed 24 February 2011].

Jancovich, Mark, Antonio Lazaro Reboll, Julian Stringer and Andrew Willis (eds) (2003), *Defining Cult Movies: The Cultural Politics of Oppositional Taste*. Manchester: Manchester University Press.

Jansen, Sue Curry (1991) *Censorship: The Knot That Binds Power and Knowledge*. Oxford: Oxford University Press.

Jarecki, Nicholas (2001) *Breaking In: How 20 Film Directors Got Their Start*. New York: Broadway Books.

Kermode, Mark (1995) 'The Case for Uncensored Cinema', *Scapegoat*, January/February, pp. 39–42.

Kermode, Mark (2002) 'The British Censor and Horror Cinema' in Steve Chibnall and Julian Petley (eds) *British Horror Cinema.* London: Routledge.

Kimber, Shaun (2000) *'Looking beyond the Obvious': The Censorship of Film Violence within Contemporary Britain.* Unpublished PhD thesis. Sheffield University.

Kinder, Marsha (2001) 'Violence American Style: The Narrative Orchestration of Violent Attractions' in David J. Slocum (ed.) *Violence and American Cinema.* London: Routledge.

King, Geoff. (2004) ' "Killingly Funny": Mixing Modalities in New Hollywood's Comedy-with-Violence' in Steven Jay Schneider (ed.) *New Hollywood Violence.* Manchester: Manchester University Press, pp. 126–43.

King, Geoff (2005) *American Independent Cinema.* London: I. B. Tauris.

King, Geoff (2007) *Donnie Darko.* London: Wallflower Press.

Kuhn, Annette (1988) *Cinema, Censorship and Sexuality 1909–1925.* London: Routledge.

Lindsey, John (2006) 'A Brilliant Shocker'. Available from: http://www.imdb.com/title/tt0099763/usercomments?filter=chrono;start=20 [accessed 10 December 2008].

lizcarran (2007) 'Extremely Disturbing'. Available from: http://www.imdb.com/title/tt0099763/usercomments?filter=chrono;start=20 [accessed 10 December 2008].

Lyons, Charles (1997) *The New Censors: Movies and the Culture Wars.* Philadelphia, PA: Temple University Press.

Male, Andrew (1997) '100 Years' Gore', *Neon*, September 1997, pp. 30–3.

Marriott, James (2004) *Horror Films.* London: Virgin Books.

Marriott, James and Kim Newman (2006) *Horror: The Definitive Guide to the Cinema of Fear.* London: André Deutsch.

Mathews, Tom Dewe (1994) *Censored: The Story of Film Censorship in Britain.* London: Chatto & Windus.

McDonough, John (1991) 'Director without a Past', *American Film*, May, pp. 42–5, 49.

McKee, Marty (2008) '*Henry: Portrait of a Serial Killer* – The 15-Years-Later Affair'. Available from: http://craneshot.blogspot.com/2008/05/henry-portrait-of-serial-killerthe-15.html [accessed 5 August 2008].

McKinney, Devin (1993) 'Violence: The Strong and the Weak', *Film Quarterly* vol. 46 no. 4, Summer, pp. 16–22.

McNaughton, John (2003a) 'Touch of Evil', *Guardian*, 25 April. Available from: http://arts.guardian.co.uk/fridayreview/story/0,,942573,00.html [accessed 20 November 2007].

McNaughton, John (2003b) Audio commentary on the Optimum Releasing DVD of *Henry: Portrait of a Serial Killer*.

McNaughton, John and Nigel Floyd (2003c) 'A Discussion of the Altered Scenes', supplementary material on the Optimum Releasing DVD of *Henry: Portrait of a Serial Killer*.

McNaughton, John and David Gregory (2005a) Audio commentary on the 20th Anniversary Special Edition DVD of *Henry: Portrait of a Serial Killer*. Orland Park, IL: Dark Sky Films.

McNaughton, John and David Gregory (2005b) 'Commentary on Deleted Scenes and Outtakes', supplementary material on the 20th Anniversary Special Edition DVD of *Henry: Portrait of a Serial Killer*. Orland Park, IL: Dark Sky Films.

Melon Farmers (2008) 'BBFC Cuts: *Henry Portrait of a Serial Killer*'. Available from: http://www.melonfarmers.co.uk/hitsh.htm [accessed 10 August 2007].

Mendik, Xavier and Graeme Harper (eds) (2000) *Unruly Pleasures: The Cult Film and Its Critics*. Guildford: FAB Press.

Morrison, David E. *et al*. (1999) *Defining Violence: The Search for Understanding*. Luton: Luton University Press.

Murdock, Graham (1997) 'Reservoirs of Dogma: An Archaeology of Popular Anxieties' in Martin Barker and Julian Petley (eds) *Ill Effects: The Media/Violence Debate*. London: Routledge, pp. 67–86.

Newman, Kim (1991) '*Henry: Portrait of a Serial Killer*', *Sight and Sound*, July 1991, pp. 43–4.

Parello, Chuck (2002) 'Interview with Chuck Parello', supplementary material on Dutch Film Works (DFW) special double disc release of *Henry: Portrait of a Serial Killer Parts 1 and 2*.

Pence, Jeffrey S. (1994) 'Terror Incognito: Representation, Repetition, Experience in *Henry Portrait of a Serial Killer*', *Public Culture* no. 6, pp. 525–45.

Petley, Julian (1997) 'Us and Them' in Martin Barker and Julian Petley (eds) *Ill Effects: The Media/Violence Debate*. London: Routledge.

Pinedo, Isabel Cristina (1997) *Recreational Terror: Women and the Pleasures of Horror Film Viewing*. Albany: State University of New York Press.

Potter, W. James (1999) *On Media Violence*. London: Sage.

Prince, Stephen (ed.) (2000) *Screening Violence*. London: Athlone Press.

rbsv (2004) 'Chilling', IMDB user reviews. Available from: http://www.imdb.com/title/tt0099763/usercomments?filter=chrono;start=20 [accessed 10 December 2008].

Readman, Mark (2005) *Teaching Film Censorship and Controversy*. London: BFI.

Rubin, Martin (1992) 'The Grayness of Darkness: *The Honeymoon Killers* and Its Impact on Psychokiller Cinema', *The Velvet Light Trap* no. 30, Fall 1992, pp. 48–64.

Schneider, Steven Jay (2009) (ed.) *1001 Horror Movies You Must See before You Die*. London: Cassell.

Sconce, Jeffrey (1993) 'Spectacles of Death: Identification, Reflexivity, and Contemporary Horror' in Jim Collins, Hilary Radner and Ava Preacher-Collins (eds) *Film Theory Goes to the Movies*. London and New York: AFI/Routledge, pp. 103–20.

Sharrett, Christopher (ed.) (1999) *Mythologies of Violence in Postmodern Media*. Detroit, MI: Wayne State University Press.

Simpson, Philip L. (2000) *Psycho Paths: Tracking the Serial Killer through Contemporary American Film and Fiction*. Carbondale: Southern Illinois University Press.

Taubin, Amy (1991) 'Killing Men', *Sight and Sound*, May, pp. 14–19.

Thompson, Kenneth A. (ed.) (1997) *Media and Cultural Regulation*. London: Sage.

Tudor, Andrew (1989) *Monsters and Mad Scientists: A Cultural History of the Horror Movie*. Oxford: Basil Blackwell.

Turner, Graeme (ed.) (2002) *The Film Cultures Reader*. London: Routledge.

Index